STEM-Rich
Maker Learning
DESIGNING FOR EQUITY WITH YOUTH OF COLOR

Angela Calabrese Barton
Edna Tan

Foreword by Yasmin B. Kafai

TEACHERS COLLEGE PRESS

TEACHERS COLLEGE | COLUMBIA UNIVERSITY
NEW YORK AND LONDON

Published by Teachers College Press, 1234 Amsterdam Avenue, New York, NY 10027

Cover design by Holly Grundon / BHG Graphic Design. Photograph by Angela Calabrese Barton.

Library of Congress Cataloging-in-Publication Data is available at loc.gov

Names: Calabrese Barton, Angela, author. l Tan, Edna, author.
Title: STEM-rich maker learning : designing for equity with youth of color / Angela Calabrese Barton, Edna Tan.
Description: New York : Teachers College Press, [2018] l Includes bibliographical references and index.
Identifiers: LCCN 2018017418
ISBN 9780807759233 (pbk. : alk. paper)
ISBN 9780807759240 (hardcover : alk. paper)
Subjects: LCSH: Maker movement in education—Social aspects—United States. l Minority youth—Education--United States. l Educational equalization—United States.
Classification: LCC LB1029.M35 C35 2018 l DDC 371.829/0835--dc23
LC record available at https://lccn.loc.gov/2018017418

ISBN 978-0-8077-5923-3 (paper)
ISBN 978-0-8077-5924-0 (hardcover)
ISBN 978-0-8077-7705-3 (ebook)

Printed on acid-free paper
Manufactured in the United States of America

25 24 23 22 21 20 19 18   8 7 6 5 4 3 2 1

Foreword

MAKING, AND NOT MAKEING

Imagine these images on the covers of *Make:* magazine, the flagship publication of the maker movement:

- A backpack equipped with lights and an alarm that the wearer can press for help when in trouble—designed by Lisa, Tina, and Tonya (ages 11, 11, and 10)
- A wind-powered anti-bully jacket designed to make people feel safe when they walk home alone at night—made by Samuel (age 14)
- A solar-powered cellphone charging case—as imagined by Caitlyn and Quentin (ages 14 and 12)
- A page from the duct tape evolution website, featuring various reversible clothing and flower designs—developed by Alie (age 14)

These everyday objects have been reimagined and remade by their designers with ingenuity and electronics. They are not just functional but also responsive to the community, as the young designers asked for their peers' input on how best to address their needs. And the designs showcase the kind of tech savviness that we value in making—where science, engineering, and technology are pulled out of their academic siloes. But the objects described above are not the types of designs that typically grace the cover of *Make:*. Nor are Alie, Caitlyn, Lisa, Quentin, Samuel, Tina, and Tonya—many of them girls and young people of color—the kind of makers we usually see in the magazine. Instead, the publication usually features rockets, robots, and drones by White and male makers.

The lack of diversity in what is made and who is represented as a maker, and where making takes place, has led Leah Buechley and others to suggest that there is "makeing"—the version promoted by the brand—and then there is making—the high- and low-tech everyday version. The maker movement has been successful in promoting various hands-on, interest-driven, and project-based activities for STEM. But this alone is not enough to overcome the stereotypes and lack of diversity that have been persistent staples of Silicon Valley culture, where the maker movement originated.

In *STEM-Rich Maker Learning: Designing for Equity with Youth of Color*, Angela Calabrese Barton and Edna Tan provide rich and complex portraits that challenge what we mean by making, makers, and makerspaces. This timely and much-needed publication critically and constructively examines the stories of making and makers that have captured the public imagination. There is no question that the maker movement had pushed researchers, educators, and tinkerers to take more expansive views of learning. Making illustrates that learning is not just minds-on but also hands-on, that learning needs to be motivated not just by curricular goals but also by personal interests, and that learning is not just a short-term event but requires sustained engagement to be impactful.

But even with these affordances, there is a chance that the maker movement will perpetuate well-documented inequities in STEM participation unless we also consider the role of community, culture, and context in making. And it is through these considerations that Calabrese Barton and Tan provide critical and creative contributions on who can be a maker, where making is taking place, and what makerspaces can look like. Much talk about the maker movement has been dominated by 3-D printers that have become the main staple of makerspaces and the hero stories of singular projects heralding the technological savviness of young makers. We often forget the preparatory advantage that many (but not all) of these makers bring from home as well as their ready access to community resources. In order to create equitable and inclusive making, we need to understand the ecologies that situate making. *STEM-Rich Maker Learning* offers promising perspectives that we can use to design more equitable and inclusive makerspaces and more engaged maker communities.

One important contribution of this book is that it situates makers as codesigners rather than just visitors of makerspaces. All too often, the focus is on tools and technologies to signal that a different kind of learning is going on. But focusing on the material side of making doesn't address who comes to the spaces, who feels invited to stay, and what mentoring of making can look like. Calabrese Barton and Tan start out by asking learners how to create more welcoming makerspaces.

Another important contribution is how the authors reframe making as a community-oriented activity rather than one that is driven by often individual interests. By addressing the source of participants' interest in making, the authors are able to connect to broader discussions in mathematics and science education about how we can value different learners' interests and experiences. Their book provides detailed analyses of how young learners engage with making, the small and big design decisions that go into their designs, and the low and high technologies that become part of the making process.

Finally, the focus on long-term, engaged making provides another critical contribution to our understanding about the type of learning that can take place in makerspaces. All too often, making is limited to one-time experiences, leaving us with few insights about how to move beyond that first project. It is a significant challenge to support and nourish continuing interest in making activities. This book presents multiple examples of not only what youth were making and what challenges they overcame but also what kept them going. Such critical narratives have been missing from the mainstream discussions, despite their obvious importance of moving forward.

What I value most about this work is that it provides us with more than just a critique of issues in the maker movement, it also provides an inclusive vision of "making," one that democratizes makerspaces and their activities. Kudos to Calabrese Barton and Tan for turning makeing into making.

—Yasmin B. Kafai
University of Pennsylvania

CHAPTER 1

Equity and the Maker Movement

Make: movement
grassroots
in schools,
science, museum
& public library

THE PROMISE OF THE MAKER MOVEMENT

Making and the maker movement have gained increasing attention not only in the United States but also across the world. Often housed in libraries or in their own dedicated facilities, makerspaces have flourished globally, proliferating in public spaces, private domains, and increasingly gaining traction in K–12 schools as a platform to promote STEM learning and creativity (Holland, 2015; Martin, 2015). Making, and makerspaces where children, youth, and adults gather to make or create an artifact—be it a simple cardboard toy or a more complicated 3-D printed avatar character with movable limbs—is spreading in a grassroots fashion across the United States and the globe (Schrock, 2014). Youth of all ages are engaging in making across contexts, including schools, science and children museums, and public libraries. Consider the following scenarios: Three middle-school youth with their parents are huddled over a table-top at a children's museum, using tools such as screwdrivers and pliers to take apart old toasters in order to figure out how internal "electronic guts" make the toaster work; in a school makerspace, middle-schoolers are working on a project to make light-up, felt-fabric bracelets; at a community Maker Faire, parents are bringing their children to experience making as part of their weekend family activities.

The maker movement has evoked interest for its potential role in breaking down barriers to STEM learning and attainment (Martin, 2015). One current theme in the maker movement focuses on empowerment. As the CEO of *Make:* magazine states, "[Y]ou're makers of your own world. . . . Makers are in control. That's what fascinates them; that's why they do what they do. They want to figure out how things work, they want to get access to it, and they want to control it" (Dougherty, 2011). The theme of empowerment is inspiring. At the same time, it is important to ask questions about how the movement defines who makers are, what makers do, what kinds of access makers need to tools and opportunities to keep making. These questions cannot be divorced from considering the social, racial, gendered, economic, and political conditions in which particular makers are bound. Espousing an egalitarian vision of making may symbolically level the playing field, while the reality is that access and opportunities to make for some groups of the population continue to remain sporadic.

As Nascimento and Pólvora (2016) pointed out, "Maker engagements with the world can easily embrace a sense of freedom and creativity to make whatever is wanted . . . with no major calls for changes in this situation, or even no concrete attention to its social conditions and consequences" (p. 6). As the maker movement becomes codified, it is largely orienting toward individual production and consumption of new products and technologies. Maker experiences open to the public often focus on pre-set activities, with little authentic room to maneuver within the activity. The attention is on the products, not the people or the relationships formed within or across these spaces.

Who is a maker and in what context a maker is accessing and engaging in making experiences are very much products of the norms and values deeply inscribed in the physicality and territories of making spaces—where making spaces are located, what tools and materials are housed within—or the identities of the maker-mentors that inhabit that space. These norms and values are themselves born of particular intersections of social (including racial and gendered), economic, and political elements. In fact, we purposefully use the term *making spaces* over *makerspace* to call attention to how making takes shape (and the learning and trajectories of makers) always in dialectic with the dynamic culture that surrounds it, rather than only with the physical space itself.

Yet, despite growing interest in equity and making, few empirical studies of *sustained youth engagement* in *STEM-oriented making* exist. There is little empirical evidence describing how youth are supported, over time, in working toward robust STEM-rich making projects or on the outcomes of such making experiences, especially among youth from historically marginalized communities. This is the focus of our book.

BUILDING A FRAMEWORK FOR EQUITABLE AND CONSEQUENTIAL MAKER LEARNING

We are excited about the potentially broad range of youth-empowering practices the making enterprise may promote, such as supporting youth to take more risks and try out new ideas. We are in equal measure concerned about the lack of explicit attention on equity concerns that are salient to making's becoming the next democratizing educational platform. *Who* is making and how are they being supported in their efforts? *What* is being made, how, and *why*? How are outcomes of making defined and measured? How we consider these questions can position some youth as central or marginal to the maker movement.

Our purpose throughout this book is to identify the hows, whats, whys, for whom, and to what ends of equitable and consequential

[handwritten: goal of book: build framework for equity & maker learning that positively impacts youth people]

community-based STEM-rich making for youth from nondominant communities. In this text, we seek to build a framework for equity and maker learning in STEM-rich making, offering new ways for the field to think about making in ways that positively impact young people and communities. Access to and opportunities for making, though fundamental, are simply not enough. We also seek to contextualize this framework for equitable and consequential maker learning with illustrative cases, which can help guide the field. In so doing, we seek to address the question: What are the possibilities for equity-oriented STEM-rich maker learning and practice that takes place with and in community settings?

Equity Concerns in the Maker Movement

Who participates? Let us pause and consider who, actually, is engaging in making. Currently, there is little evidence that the maker movement has been *broadly successful* at involving a diverse audience, especially over a sustained period of time. There are pockets of success around the nation where makerspaces have successfully reached a more diverse population than the trending White and male spaces (e.g., the Mt. Elliott Makerspace in Detroit). Few of these more diverse makerspaces are intentionally STEM-rich. However, these spaces are the exception and not the norm. Little research has been done on these spaces to document what is working, how, or why.

The maker movement remains a largely adult, White, middle-class pursuit, led by those with the leisure time, technical knowledge, experience, and resources to make. Indeed, the demographics of both the authors and readers (89% of authors, 81% of readers have median incomes of $106,000) of *Make:* magazine (the periodical credited with launching the Maker Movement) show largely educated White males (Brahms & Crowley, 2016). This is troubling when we consider the speed and spread of makerspace proliferation across both formal and informal education contexts. The maker culture that is solidifying, if not challenged, will be one that is dominantly White, male, and middle-class, perpetuating the chronic inequities in education at large, and in STEM education in particular. Inability to identify with STEM due to a lack of role models from one's own community as well as alienating practices within STEM experiences has led to "identity gaps" (e.g., Eisenhart & Finkel, 1998; Johnson, Brown, Carlone, & Cuevas, 2011) in STEM education, where students of color are reluctant to pursue higher-level STEM courses, in spite of test scores comparable to those of their White peers. A White, male, middle-class maker culture is unlikely to ameliorate this longstanding problem. For decades, African Americans have made up less than 5% of the engineering workforce in the United States (Yoder, 2014). African Americans, Latinos, and Native Americans account for only 6% of the total STEM labor force, even though they represent over one-fourth of the U.S. population (National Science Foundation, 2014).

[handwritten margin note: youth don't have STEM role models ↓ leads to identity gaps]

Participation and the Culture of Making

There is little evidence that the *dominant culture* of the maker movement, as described above, has been broadly shaped by a diverse audience over a sustained period of time. Thus, as the maker movement has become formalized, the powerful knowledge, practices, and collective wisdom of communities of color or of low-income communities have not yet become central to its discourse.

Furthermore, making that youth deem consequential to their lives or how such learning or making is supported is not well understood. Most making resources directed toward children promote the "keychain syndrome"—a reference to youth going to a makerspace and 3-D printing a preformatted keychain. These kinds of making experiences are often trivial and do not involve prolonged or sustained meaningful engagement or anticipation of more complex projects (Blikstein & Worsley, 2016).

The maker movement has paid scant attention to sustained maker learning experiences, despite recent acknowledgment of the importance of such in deepening knowledge and practice in STEM (ASEE, 2016). Even when making projects support authentic engagement on a problem one cares about, there has been limited critical engagement with what constitutes consequentiality in making or for whom. For example, the projects in *Make:* magazine seldom have a community focus. When they do, there is little attention beyond the normative family unit or peer group (again mostly middle class, and mostly White). Little attention is paid to intersections of family with history, location, or a more expanded community. What constitutes community has not been a focal question in making, and yet we think our study reported on here uncovers the importance of layers of community across people, space, and time.

The shift toward *culture* is significant from an equity standpoint: Whose voices are valued and who counts as legitimate participants in a community making space impact how various people are welcomed, positioned, and recognized for what they know and can do as a part of shaping the learning and participation that happens there. As we consider a *culture of making*, we are particularly interested in the relationships among "I, Thou, and It"—the teacher, the child, and the world around them (Hawkins, 1974), and what those relationships mean for being together in a space. How people are welcomed, positioned, and recognized for what they know and can do in a making space shapes the culture of learning and participation that happens there. Making space educators and participants can be co-constructors of culture, engaged in mutual activity that can maintain and challenge normative views of knowledge production and expertise. Examining how an emergent maker culture is actively shaped in community is a productive way to unpack how youth's diverse interests and the historicized practices of communities of color are rich and legitimate resources for making.

Why Focus on Equity in STEM-Rich Making?

Some critics warn against the danger of conflating making with STEM, worrying that questions about learning in making will "become synonymous with 'Where is the STEM in making?'" (Vossoughi, Hooper, & Escude, 2016).

In framing equity in making in this book, we situate STEM squarely in the center of making and argue that STEM cannot be divorced from making if equity is the goal. For youth of color and girls who have been traditionally underrepresented in STEM, making can be a productive and empowering platform for them to get a foothold into STEM through authentic, STEM-rich making experiences. While we do not hold the position that youth of color should all be encouraged into STEM pathways, nor do we hold a singular view of what STEM engagement may be, we do take seriously the grave issue that youth of color growing up in low-income communities have been chronically underserved by society in their access to, and consistent opportunities to engage in, rich STEM experiences.

At the same time, we acknowledge the unique status with which STEM disciplines are regarded in society. This is a double-edged sword. Success in STEM is one viable route toward personal and community economic advancement for youth growing up in poverty. Success in STEM also factors into opportunities for empowered democratic participation. Indeed, one who is well endowed with STEM competencies is better positioned to make socio-scientific decisions in his or her life that can have far-reaching consequences, such as in health care and access to clean water and air. That lower-income communities of color experience the greatest levels of environmental injustice and often have the least voice in STEM-related decisions affecting their communities is further evidence of the impact of these persistent inequities (National Academy of Engineering, 2010).

Yet, at the same time, participation in STEM can be a marginalizing experience. The culture—and thus the knowledge and practices—of STEM is grounded in dominant White, male culture, and youth are expected to assimilate this culture. Without explicit disruption, expectations around forms of participation may lead to a deficit orientation toward nondominant forms of knowledge and practice, which can further position youth as outsiders to STEM-rich making.

We further recognize that there is a wide range of making projects that are not overtly STEM-oriented, such as cooking or embroidery, although they could be. However, we focus on STEM-rich making precisely because STEM is a domain to which many youth from historically marginalized communities have been denied equitable access, and because the making movement claims to reduce barriers to access and opportunity in STEM.

However, we focus on STEM-rich making because we are interested to learn more about making projects and experiences that support makers in deepening and applying science and engineering knowledge and practice, *in synergy with* other powerful forms of knowledge and practice, such as the funds of knowledge (Gonzáles, Moll, & Amanti, 2006) and community wisdom (Tuck, 2009) one has because of who one is, and where one has grown up. We are interested when such synergies allow for disruptions of expectations for what STEM-rich may mean in making. For example, there is a growing focus on the role of e-textiles (e.g., light-up fashionwear) in supporting youth makers in learning to code simple microcontrollers and to build circuits while also drawing upon knowledge of sewing and fashion (Kafai, Fields, & Searle, 2014). Bang, Marin, Faber, and Suzukovich (2013) discuss the importance of repatriating and innovating technologies in STEM-related work with Indigenous youth to "dislodge" such technologies from colonial legacies. This is another way to think about culture and equity in STEM-rich making, because it shows how technology can be reconstructed toward new purposes and grounded in sustaining knowledge systems, repositioning youth as "makers" rather than "consumers" of technology.

Advancing Equity   ~ but what & equity; is it only access + opportunity

The idea that STEM-rich making may promote more equitable opportunities for learning and becoming in STEM is widely accepted. However, there is little agreement on what equity means or what the goals of equity should be in maker learning. As maker educators and researchers, we are invested in finding ways to support maker learning in ways that map onto, but also help to transform, the maker movement.

Within the field of making, equity has primarily been framed in terms of access and opportunity. Within this framing, important questions are being asked, such as: Where is making happening? What is the quality of maker mentoring or maker pedagogies? For example, some studies have documented the importance of maker educators or mentors asking questions rather than giving answers, encouraging exploration and failure, making thinking transparent, or being a connector for youth and ideas and tools (Ryoo, Bulalacao, Kekelis, McLeod, & Henriquez, 2015). Such practices promote equity goals because they have been shown to promote greater success in making and the negotiation of gendered and racialized identities in making (Norris, 2014). How these practices are tied to a culture of making is underexplored.

However, and importantly, studies are emerging that are critically expanding the discourse on access and opportunity, raising questions about cultural narratives that drive making opportunities. For example, Vossoughi and her colleagues (2016) remind us the maker movement tends to value forms and outcomes of making that are representative of

[handwritten margin note at top: → issue of equity that is addressed, not normally have access, once they are forced to write kids assimilate culture which isn't equitable]

normative White culture, though we would add that middle-class and school-educated class values are strongly reflected in this normative culture as well. In response to these narratives, approaches to equity should include both a critical analysis of the injustices that youth makers have experiences in, as a part of promoting historicized approaches to making. Such an equity approach also frames making as a cross-cultural activity, with inquiry into the sociopolitical values and purposes of making.

We also assert that most equity discourses in maker education focus at the individual level—on who is making, whether or how that person may or may not fit into the culture of making, or how to best support makers in achieving their own goals through pedagogies and mentoring. Such approaches may improve individual youth's access and opportunity, but they do not necessarily, or at least directly, call attention to the ways in which historicized injustice manifests in the systems of power that play out in the maker movement. Equity discourses that shift from "fixing" the individual to re-mediating and transforming the system are key to reimagining an equity-oriented approach to maker learning.

Still, much more work is needed in fleshing out a stance on equity in making. If we are to promote real and sustained change for youth makers and their mentors, we need to build more robust theories of equity in making that attend to intersecting scales of injustice. Toward that effort, we consider two broad dimensions: *equitable* and *consequential*.

By *equitable*, we suggest that it is imperative that youth have empowering opportunities to engage in STEM in culturally sustaining and rigorous ways. Here we are concerned with opportunities for young people to deepen STEM and making knowledges/practices as a part of, not separate from, their own cultural knowledge and making practices. We are also concerned that young people have opportunities to connect STEM-rich making with their community and broader social issues that matter to them locally, with understandings of how these concerns may connect to broader systemic issues. This would involve supporting the practices and culture of youth makers and community-based making that acknowledge the sociohistorical realities that young people face, and their wisdom and agency toward social transformation for which they seek support and recognition through their making efforts (Yosso, 2005). As Tuck (2009) reminds us, "desire-based research frameworks" require epistemological shifts accounting for "the loss and despair, but also the hope, the visions, the wisdom of lived lives and communities. Desire is involved with the *not yet* and, at times, the *not anymore*" (p. 417). In short, we view *equitable* here as supporting and promoting the knowledge and practices that enable youth's agentic response to desires of the *not yet* and their efforts to reclaim the *not anymore*.

[handwritten margin note: equitable def.]

[handwritten margin note: making should be part of a person's own cultural knowledge + practices + relate to broader issues in their community]

By *consequential*, we suggest that making opportunities leverage upon advancing STEM learning and participation toward transformative outcomes aimed at addressing systemic inequalities, such as supporting youth

[handwritten margin note: consequential def.]

agency to make in ways that matter to them and their communities while also disrupting power dynamics in STEM and in making. Other transformative outcomes include expanding youth's social networks for making in ways that promote greater inclusivity through engaging with a wider range of participants (e.g., peers, families, community, STEM experts), and viewing making as happening across scales of activity—such as how making involves local projects that project new discourses onto the field.

In considering *equitable* and *consequential* making for youth, we want to interrogate what it means for youth growing up in lower-income communities, especially youth of color, to engage in *sustained* making experiences in ways that position them as competent youth with valuable experiences and ideas of their own, value their identities as youth of color, and at the same time support their growing STEM and making expertise during the process.

As we will discuss across this text, the focus on sustained engagement is significant. Increasing STEM knowledge and practice in ways that can be transformed by community knowledge and experience takes time. If equity is to be centrally prioritized in the maker movement, then explicit and ongoing attention needs to be paid to youth's whole lives, including the community knowledge and wealth they bring to making alongside the systemic injustices that youth face in making and in the world. This stance builds on work in the learning sciences on teaching and learning as relational and historicized activities, by pushing beyond the focus on individual learners to also address how systemic injustices intersect with classroom practice.

they came up w/ solve
? this is a problem of their idea to own
a problem of their own

LIGHT-UP SCOOTER

— 2 5th grade girls made a scooter that lights up so they could ride it after dark

To gain deeper insights of how we are framing *equitable* and *consequential* we share a brief vignette about Jennifer and Emily. Both girls joined their local community-based maker program in the 5th grade. Jennifer joined because she wanted to use the computers that she knew the club had. She thought that "science is boring," and often complained that she was not allowed to "build" things or "use technology" in school science. However, she felt that she was good at using the computer and the Internet, and the community making club would give her a chance to learn new skills. More often than not, outside of school, Jennifer felt that no one recognized her interest or ability with technology. For example, when teachers asked questions about computer skills and the Internet during class, Jennifer was the first one to raise her hand to answer the questions, even though she was rarely called on to help. Her expertise in technology was also not encouraged at home. For example, Jennifer was interested in jailbreaking the iPhone, and she tried to jailbreak her mom's phone several times:

> *Jennifer:* I am good at jailbreaking stuff. I am actually good at jailbreaking. Like going on an iPad or iPod or whatever, it's like an unlock. You can jailbreak it and get inside of it.
> *Interviewer:* Ah, did you try it?
> *Jennifer:* My mom's iPhone. I read her emails [laughs].

Emily, on the other hand, joined because Jennifer joined. The two were best friends, and had been from an early age. They both came to the local community club most days after school because both had mothers who worked in the after-school hours, and their schools did not provide after-school programs. Emily felt that the program gave her something to do with her friend that was interesting.

Together, the two girls designed, built, and refined a solar-powered light-up scooter with rechargeable batteries. The lights included a small set of LED holiday lights brought in by one of their mentors, hacked to fit their scooter and to be powered by a solar panel. The lights were decoratively wrapped around the stem and handle bars, making the lights visible, but away from the mechanisms that made the scooter work. The solar panel included two 5V panels stitched together and affixed to the top of the handlebars. There was also a switch for turning the lights on and off.

They designed their scooter because both they and their peers were unable to play with their scooters or travel to one another's homes after dark because of the limited number of streetlights in their neighborhood. They each owned a small kick-style scooter, and scooters were cool. "Everyone has one":

> *Researcher:* Why did you try to make something new using the scooters?
> *Emily:* Scooters are cool. Scooters are just cool; they're cool.
> *Researcher:* How did you know that?
> *Jennifer:* A lot of kids own scooters.

Though straightforward in design, the scooter took several months of design iterations for it to work the way the girls wished.

It took about 6 weeks for the girls to settle on this particular idea. Though they knew they wanted to solve their transportation problem, they originally wanted to make an electric scooter so that they could get to places more quickly. As Emily said: "Speed is important to me . . . the kick scooter is one of the ones where you have to, like, push yourself. They are not like the motorized. So as far as speed and everything like that, we were looking more just for operations for getting things moving." They were also concerned with how the electric scooter might help people "save on gas."

The scooter would also have a phone dock (for the "10-, 12-year-olds who probably do have phones") as well as "soft handlebars" to make the ride comfortable (see sketch, Figure 1.1). The scooter would be adjustable in size to meet a wide range of ages, and would have a button on the handlebars to allow the user to "accelerate" in case you need to "get away" from something. As they further described in their interview:

> Well, it kind of entertains kids, and adults can ride it. For little kids, there's streamer things on it, so you could just attach the streamers or take them off if you don't want them on or not. You can get them in different colors. It kind of helps parents, like when they're going somewhere, and they leave their kid with someone at home, and they're like a troubled kid. You want to buy something for them so it entertains them so the people who watch them don't have as much trouble as having to be in a house all day hearing them scream, yell, and break things. It keeps them entertained, and it also gives them exercise because your leg is moving, and it's pushing you. You're pushing yourself.

However, after collecting survey, observational, and interview data about who uses scooters and when, and what their transportation concerns were, they noticed in the survey data that people were less worried about saving gas "because they don't have a car." But they also noticed that people did not want to have to pay extra to power the scooter, either. The survey data also presented new challenges the girls had not thought of, related to winter transportation. Not only were they challenged to consider how the scooter might work in snow and mud, but they were also challenged by the safety issue of being able to see and be seen in the dark. The girls also noticed, through their observations, that most kids had a kick scooter.

The girls decided to modify their design to make a "light up" kick scooter. They decided to add "lights" because their peers noted that people needed to be able to "see you." They also decided that the kick style, especially if modified to have "special wheels," would "have a chance against the snow or mud." They decided to add "padding so if you fall and you fall on the scooter the fall isn't so hard." Lastly, they decided on a solar panel so that people could "save money" in powering the lights.

This process was highly iterative in terms of the technical and social dimensions of the designs; it required ongoing input from peers, community members, and STEM and making experts so that it worked, given their particular needs and experiences in the world. When they and their mentor ran into problems trying to figure out how to hack the LED "holiday lights" their mentor brought in from home, the girls went onto YouTube to find solutions for how to solve their problem. Again, as Jennifer

Figure 1.1. Sketch of Electric Scooter

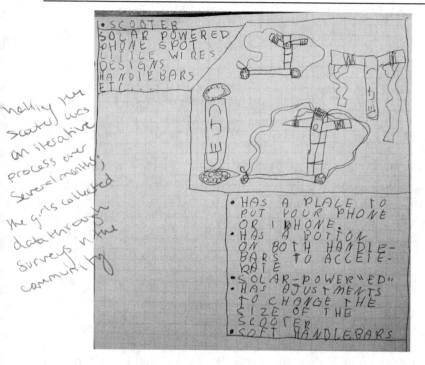

explained: "There's a lot of stuff I got on YouTube . . . that we got on You-Tube for hooking up the things and copper ball and everything we got off YouTube. I'm actually really good with YouTube, actually."

When they could not power the lights as brightly as they wished with their solar panel, they recalled stories about the sun from school, and sought out help from a science teacher at a "feedback cycle" event hosted by their making club. Jennifer explained, recalling that the angle of the sun was so low in the winter, they had to consider how to angle the solar panel on their scooter:

Yeah, but in our science class we're learning about how the sunrise and the sunset and the sun angle and stuff can be very different. In the winter, the daytime, the daylight is way shorter because in the winter it's really dark. Probably like at 5 or 4 it gets super dark. It starts getting really dark, and the sun starts to fade away more and more. Even in the morning it's dark. . . . Actually, before we met the [feedback cycle experts], they were actually, I just looked down here and they were the ones who told us to have a solar panel that faces up and down and we needed a bigger one . . . and that it needed to be 45 degrees, yeah, because before we had it smaller.

But, even after solving this problem with the help of some outside experts, they ran into further problems because the solar panel did not work in the dark or on cloudy days. They had to turn to their own ideas and help from their peers, and they decided to incorporate rechargeable batteries.

When the girls finally got their design to work they were ecstatic (Figure 1.2). They brought the completed project to school to share with their friends at recess: "Recess, yeah, because how to have fun with this helped us think of this because we're kids and recess." Jennifer summed up their feelings when she said what the scooter would say about them:

> It would probably say this girl knows how to have fun, how to get down and smart when she really needs to. It will probably say about me, she knows how to have fun. She can get down and smart when she really needs to. This girl can be fun. She could build things. She could make the world a different place and help everybody else learn how to have the type of fun she has and stuff.

We view Jennifer and Emily's making process, which took months, as both equitable and consequential. The girls engaged in making as community insiders who were making for a specific purpose—to solve a real problem many of them face as young people living in a town with a severe lack of streetlights. From conceptualizing the problem-space to the final production of their functional scooter prototype, the girls had continual, free, weekly access to a community making space staffed by consistent maker-mentors, who provided technical expertise, including project guidance and relevant STEM instruction, when needed. Collaboratively, the girls sought relevant social data through interviews and conversations with community members and peers. What they made was not born out of benign, hobbyist interest, but of real necessity. The resources they drew on to prototype their scooter resided beyond the walls of the makerspace to include community data. As Nasir, Rosebery, Warren, and Lee (2014) argued, a deep sense of social belonging is a key marker of equitable learning environments. What the youth chose to make, why, and how were all girded in and informed by their everyday identities, experiences, and particular challenges.

They also brought to bear community challenges such as lack of transportation for themselves and many of their peers due to infrequent bus schedules and constrained family resources. They noted the lack of streetlights in their neighborhoods, which is an important safety concern when a youth is commuting on his or her own on a scooter. They were also concerned with social aspects important to youth—the scooter features had to be appealing to them and their friends. Their use of a large solar panel to charge the lights reflected their understanding of both

Figure 1.2. Final Light-up Scooter

What's better? This scooter has a solar panel!

environmental and financial issues relevant to their innovation. These insights are drawn from their embodied experiences through community engagement in their everyday lives. Innovating the light-up scooter attended to equitable elements through the robust STEM-rich making experiences Emily and Jennifer experienced, requiring them to learn more about circuits, energy sources, and transformations, and storage. Making the scooter was consequential because it addressed an immediate community need in a tangible ways, while acknowledging the girls' emerging standing as community youth makers.

LEARNING WITH YOUTH: THE CHAPTERS IN THIS BOOK

This book is made up of eight chapters, which we conceptually group into three sections: Framing Equity, Design Principles of Equity in STEM-rich Making, and Transformative Outcomes. We describe the chapters in each section.

In Chapter 1 we have worked to make the case for why equity matters in STEM-rich making, and have presented the salient factors pertaining to equity that need to be parsed out. We have argued for equity in STEM-rich making to be constituted of *equitable* and *consequential* outcomes. Chapter 2 builds on this argument through introducing a framework that expands upon and undergirds these ideals with literature on the sociocultural dimensions of learning and critical justice. This framework, which we refer to as *Mobilities of Criticality*, highlights the importance of intersectional geometries of power in when, where, and how people learn in and through making. In this chapter we present four dimensions to this framework that highlight how embodied criticalities that youth experience as injustices in specific domains of their everyday lives (be it the lack of warm clothing in winter due to poverty, or the fear of bullying in school) are fluid and can be translocated and addressed in a making space domain. We theorize the relationships between youths' multiple identities (e.g., STEM learner, young person, African American, female, marginalized school science student, and insider–community member) and the norms and culture of a community-based making space that can facilitate such Mobilities of Criticality toward advancing the equity agenda.

Design Principles for Equity in Making

In Chapters 3, 4, and 5 we develop in some detail six key design principles that we believe help to promote equitable and consequential STEM-rich making: (1) participatory methodologies for maker teaching, learning, sharing, and research; (2) considering and operationalizing porous boundaries; (3) equipping youth with insider ethnographic knowledge and practice; (4) elevating voices and expanding roles of youth and community throughout the making process; (5) supporting new models of making including co-making and justice-oriented making—with whom, using what resources, toward what ends; and (6) engaging in community-identified just-in-time STEM experiences.

Chapter 3 examines the role and importance of participatory methodologies and pedagogies alongside the importance of elevating youth voices and roles, and porous boundaries. Authored with the youth, this chapter examines their efforts to engage in an extended Youth Participatory Action Research (YPAR) project where they sought to design their own making space and culture that legitimately welcomed them, while extending them outward to their communities. We leverage the youth's experiences and ways of looking at making spaces to examine the research focused on the design of youth-centered making spaces, raising questions about what it means to be a fully welcomed member of a making space. Their story illustrates how they worked to challenge the traditional boundaries of making and makerspaces while seeking to re-create their own making spaces with multilayered meanings—meanings tied to who the youth are, who they want to be, and what they want to do in these spaces.

Chapter 4 explores the roles youth makers play as community ethnographers, which underpins their making actions when designing and prototyping innovations that will "help the community." First, we describe the different ways in which community as ethnography is taken up in the two partner sites. Then we explore how youth making takes shape, over time, as they engaged, in sustained ways, with community, STEM, and making, as they sought to make sense of and improve upon both the technical and social dimensions of their designs. We further argue that youth participatory ethnography as pedagogical practice repositioned youth and making by challenging the boundaries that inscribe STEM-rich maker knowledge and practice.

In Chapter 5 we develop the design principle of co-making to draw attention to norms and routines that create spaces for and help legitimize input from many different people across time and settings. This includes youth codeveloping criteria for making projects/progress; valuing student and community members' input toward shaping project process and outcomes; encouraging project work to occur in many different places and drawing upon the resources in the places; spending large chunks of time on supporting youth in negotiating their own ideas with others, and sharing ownership of the making process and project. Looking across more than 40 maker projects, which youth co-made over months and, in some cases, years, we first describe how both community ethnography and just-in-time STEM enabled and supported a practice of co-making. Then we examine how co-making through community ethnography contributed to more porous boundaries, expanding opportunities for youth to grow their social networks, and to be recognized for their efforts across communities of practice. We also discuss how co-making helped reorganize traditional knowledge/power hierarchies, challenging views of what it means to be an expert STEM-rich maker.

Transformative Outcomes

Chapter 6 looks at how youth's STEM-rich making worked to make a difference in their lives and in their communities, challenging both local practices regarding who can make and what making looks like, and systemic inequalities they experience in their lives and communities. To do so, we present in-depth stories of youth makers. First, we tell the story of Samuel, a young African American boy, and his design of an LED light-up football for his peers to play with in a neighborhood with no streetlights. Second, we tell the story of Emily and Jennifer's heated jacket, meant to keep themselves and their peers warm on cold days, and to prevent bullying due to old clothes. In telling these stories, we argue that through their making practice these young people are involved not only in "artifact making" (the prototypically viewed outcome of makerspace work), but also in place-making within and across the worlds of STEM, makerspaces, and community. Such place-making fosters new forms of interaction among scales of activity, and supports the movement of ideas, resources, relationships, and people in support of youth's emerging practices and how they might be recognized for them. As the youth engage in their making practices, they inscribe new meanings for what they are doing when they make within the places they inhabit, refiguring participation in these places and the possibilities for becoming within them.

Chapter 7 examines how opportunities to engage in equitable and consequential making support youth in expanding both their agency and their community youth maker practices. In this chapter, we take up the ways in which youth *spread* access and opportunity in making within their community—and as mediated by the youth's culture and sociohistorical context. In particular, we explore what we refer to as "community youth maker practices" that youth cocreate as they seek to spread and grow the reach of their making efforts into their community, and to equip their community with STEM-rich maker practices that draw strength from community knowledge and practice. To make sense of these ideas, we present two critical events—an electric art workshop and a stop-motion animation workshop, both activities prepared by youth over months, and offered to members of their local communities. These two workshops were designed and enacted by youth to sharing their developing STEM-rich making expertise through teaching other youth at their community clubs.

We return to our framework, Mobilites of Criticalities, in Chapter 8. Looking across the chapters, we discuss how maker learning, when understood through the Mobilities of Criticality framework, can show how youth make from an intersectional stance, drawing from various experiences in their everyday lives. Youth's progress and negotiations in becoming "youth community makers," with the attendant obstacles, tensions, and significant identity "lamination" moments, will be discussed. We reiterate the key arguments laid forth in the previous chapters and conclude with a discussion of the elements in a making program and learning environment committed to being equitably consequential for the nation's underserved youth.

LOOKING AHEAD

In this chapter, we suggest that to promote a more equitable and consequential maker culture for youth of color, we need to call attention to the importance of providing empowering opportunities for students to engage with making in culturally sustaining and rigorous ways, and in how such opportunities may promote transformative outcomes aimed at addressing systemic inequalities, such as critical agency and shifting power dynamics. We are concerned with how youth's making practice takes shape across multiple scales of activity as well as over time (e.g., locally among peers in small-group work as well as in the real and imagined places of STEM). Thus, we feel that if equity is to be centrally prioritized in the maker movement, explicit attention needs to be paid to youth's whole lives, including the community knowledge and wealth they bring to making alongside the systemic injustices that youth face in making and in the world. In the next chapter we build on these ideas to offer a framework for making sense of equity-oriented maker learning —Mobilities of Criticality.

CHAPTER 2

Working Toward an Equitable and Consequential Culture of Youth-Based Maker Learning

FEELING ACCOMPLISHED

I think it is important for kids to have the opportunity to feel accomplished with what they are working on. By keeping working on their projects and making it into a bigger better project kids could help make a difference, and they could become famous for what they are doing. In electric art, kids felt accomplished with the games that they made, and how they helped other kids learn to make them, too. Basically, it's about what you learned, how you worked on it, and how others saw it and what it meant to them.

I felt accomplished in my maker club a lot of times. It could be like the Little Free STEM Library (LFL) because that is the first thing that came to mind because it's in front of my face. Last year, when we went to the [entrepreneur] event, Samuel and I had gotten business cards from people because people wanted us to build more LFLs and put them around the city. I felt accomplished because I didn't think people would give us business cards, and they did because they wanted more LFLs. LFLs are important because they help other kids practice reading and learn more about science. If kids live in a library desert like us, it really matters more.

This is different from school because at school some teachers make you feel that you can't be accomplished in life. Here I feel the opposite because we get to make different projects, and at school we don't get to do it.

It does matter in the community because your projects could go further into different communities. If we were over in the south side where I live, people would be like that is cool, but we could go to the east side and they could learn, too. They could learn and make a difference, too! Then they would reach

[handwritten margin note:] LFLS: STEM Libraries located in library deserts — use to help kids practice reading + learn science

out to other communities, and it would just keep growing and growing. . . . —Fall, Chief Club Blogger

in poverty but still has made it

Fall has been involved in her community-based making space for many years. Over her time in her maker club, she has made a Little Free STEM Library, videos, and other digital artifacts educating others about energy- and money-saving technologies in the home, the significance of food and library deserts in her community and how to map them, and the role of green energy in her community. She has also mentored countless other youth on their projects, ranging from a light-up umbrella and a heated jacket to smartphone apps focused on teaching others about the foster system and bullying. She appointed herself the "chief blogger" for her club.

In her blog post above, she describes the importance of "working on projects . . . to make a difference" in her own community, but also spreading those accomplishments to help other communities. She also points out the importance of being recognized for what one has accomplished in making work. Indeed, she wants to feel accomplished for what she has learned and can do and how that has made a difference to her community, and she wants others to have these same feelings. These are powerful words that capture what it could mean to learn and to become in STEM-rich making.

Because she is a young woman growing up in multigenerational poverty, these words carry even deeper meaning for Fall, as they push back against the dominant narratives about who can make, or who can make a difference. She has described these dominant narratives as hurtful to her family and friends and to herself. She has acknowledged being bullied in school because her family lacks economic resources and cannot afford the best clothes. She has described the low expectations set for her academic work and what it is like being labeled as a struggling reader. Her mom held low expectations toward her academic achievement, and because she was a well-behaved student, her teachers gave her little attention.

And yet, despite these dominant narratives, and how they have played out in her day-to-day experiences over years, Fall has established herself as a "STEM leader" in her community and an extensive blogger on STEM issues, taking up projects and concerns that push back against these oppressions she and others have faced. Her blog posts, kept across the past several years, like the post above, remind the world of how hard she and her peers have worked, how important access to STEM is, how important the maker projects they make are, and how much others appreciate their work. She points to the importance of STEM knowledge and to knowledge of community as crucial in their projects, and crucial in helping other youth like her "get to where [she] has gotten."

Fall's blog post, which reflects her STEM-rich maker learning and becoming, suggests that we need to develop more robust understandings of how, when, and why youth seek to learn and to become in STEM-rich making in ways that matter to themselves, their communities, and the maker movement.

CONSIDERING EQUITABLE AND CONSEQUENTIAL MAKER LEARNING: MOBILITIES OF CRITICALITY

As maker educators and researchers, we are invested in finding ways to support *equitable* and *consequential* maker learning, in ways that map onto, but also help to transform, the maker movement. But what does it mean to bring an explicit equity stance to sociocultural views of maker learning? We use the phrase *Mobilities of Criticality* to call attention to how maker learning in-practice involves critical engagement with "the word and the world" (Freire, 1970) as a part of how individuals participate in practice across spaces and time.

We ground our framework in two domains: critical justice studies and sociocultural views of learning. As we noted in Chapter 1, there is little agreement on what equity means or what the goals of equity should be in making. Who is making, and where do they get access to the tools, resources, and opportunities to make? However, there is little interrogation beyond these ideals. This distributive view of equity, grounded in a liberal political view of equality (Rawls, 1971), implies a sense of impartiality (Young, 1990). Yet we see this stance echoed in the maker movement: Broader access to makerspaces, materials, and mentors will support more people in making.

However, access and opportunity are not neutral experiences. Within sociological studies, this view of equity includes both access to resources and the ways in which access has been historically and politically institutionalized. Few maker studies offer attention to how the cultural resources for STEM-rich making are grounded in Western ways of knowing/doing, or to the deep gaps in resources that exist across communities and contexts (Bang & Bajaras, in press).

Despite this dominant distributive view, more critically oriented views of equity have become a part of the research literature in maker education. These views of equity, which include "relational" views (Dawson, 2014), challenge the normative practices and power structures in making. Rather than focusing on equal access and opportunity, individuals' needs are taken into account in relation to who they are and what their lives are like (e.g., Kafai, et al., 2014). Honneth and Fraser (2003) remind us that the goal of recognition is to recognize need and value difference rather than to promote assimilation to the dominant culture. The relational view

(handwritten margin note: looking at equity through critical justice studies + sociocultural views of learning)

of equity points out how youth's historicized experiences may not be a part of making, and that crossing over into the dominant world of making may require youth to check these experiences at the makerspace door. The risks young people face when entering into a potentially unwelcoming world can be high. A relational view of equity reorganizes access and opportunity, situating the importance of promoting multiple points of entry and forms of movement through experiences.

Distributional and relational views of equity help uncover stark inequities in the maker movement. However, alone they are insufficient in disrupting participation boundaries and knowledge hierarchies such that full participation in maker communities is possible. Thus, in building this framework, we draw upon critical views of justice to provide conceptual tools for making sense of how systemic injustices give texture to the local practices that shape and inform maker learning and becoming, and how they might be disrupted toward more equitable and consequential ends (Balibar, Mezzadra, & Samaddar, 2012; Squire & Darling, 2013).

In particular, we seek to call attention to how individual experiences of injustice intersect with systemic injustice through sanctioned power hierarchies (Barnett, 2005). By power hierarchies, we refer to the ways individuals are recognized, valued, and positioned with status and authority—or not—as a result of sociohistorical structures and practices imbued with racism, classism, sexism, and heteronormativity. How youth are welcomed as legitimately belonging in a place is informed by the historicized injustices "outsiders" have encountered in relation to participation in place. We view legitimacy as a crucial form of validation, grounded in cultural systems and power, and allotted to place (Gonzales & Terosky, 2016). This stance on legitimacy goes beyond the sociocognitive stance, where legitimate participation is understood in terms of becoming acquainted with the practices and discourses that are central to a community as it is *already constructed* within practice (Lave & Wenger, 1991).

Power hierarchies shape life in makerspaces just as they do in classrooms, informal science programs, and other places of learning. *Who* is mentoring or learning, *what* is taught and made and *why*, and how maker success is defined and measured can position some individuals as marginal as their very starting point in maker learning, just because of who they are and what they bring to the process.

Thus, despite the espoused "democratizing effects" of making, how youth leverage their knowledge of community knowledge and wealth could still be positioned hierarchically by the teacher/adult facilitator or peers, even if such practices have a role in making. These unequal distributions of power can impact whether or not one sees oneself as capable and welcomed in STEM or making. A critical justice view of equity seeks to cultivate empowering interactions and outcomes by disrupting these power hierarchies.

Second, we ground our Mobilities of Criticality framework in sociocultural views of learning and development that places human interaction and activity at the center of analysis (Engeström & Sannino, 2010; Vossoughi & Gutiérrez, 2014). This dynamic view of learning foregrounds how people, ideas, tools, resources, bodies, and relationships move as people engage in social practice toward new futures (Leander, Phillips & Taylor, 2010; Vossoughi & Gutiérrez, 2014). It also foregrounds why it is important to make sense of youth's making practice as taking shape across multiple scales of activity as well as over time (e.g., locally among peers in small-group work as well as in the real and imagined places of STEM).

In our sociocultural stance, we hold the view that there are "no cultureless or neutral" ways of being in the world (Bang et al., 2013). Here we conceptualize culture as dynamic, yet made up of routine practices —a "usual way of doing things" through a "history of involvement"—in which individuals and communities engage, rather than reductive (and typically deficit-oriented) views framed by membership in particular groups (Gutiérrez & Rogoff, 2003, p. 21).

Bringing together critical justice studies and sociocultural learning theories makes a strong case for the importance of providing empowering opportunities for students to engage with making in sustaining and rigorous ways, while promoting transformative outcomes aimed at addressing systemic inequalities, such as critical agency and shifting power dynamics. Below, we present four interrelated domains that undergird a Mobilities of Criticality framework: movement, intersectional geometries of power, place-making, and presence.

Movement

Learning always takes place *somewhere*, both in "relation to history (time) and context (place/space)" (Bright, Manchester, & Allendyke, 2013, p. 749). As people move from place to place they bring with them ideas, tools, resources, and relationships, re-making and re-mixing them toward their interests (Leander et al., 2010). We are particularly interested in how youth connect their experiences across different youth-driven spaces, their communities, and STEM toward their own "social futures" (Gutiérrez, 2008, p. 156). Focused on more than vertical movement (e.g., such as novice to expert), a mobilities perspective illuminates how practices transform into new practices—some hybrid in form, others as re-creations—as people move from place to place and over time. Recognizing horizontal forms of movement and knowledge and practice building is important because it contributes to widening what counts as expertise by including "the negotiation of various contexts and the development of hybrid solutions" (Vossoughi & Gutiérrez, 2014, p. 610).

For example, examining the critical literacy practices of migrant youth in southern California, Gutiérrez (2008) describes how youth use their "complete linguistic toolkits"—toolkits made up of linguistic practices of home and community, such as *testimonio*, in addition to the practices that are sanctioned in school settings—to navigate "the paradoxes of migration, immigration, and schooling" in the United States (p. 150). These hybrid practices helped students link their past and present to an imagined future, and reorganize everyday concepts acquired through social interaction in the joint activities of school-based literacies. She suggests that these "rich interactional matrices of practice" lead to a new dialectic between "the world as it is and the world as it could be," opening up new places for learning and transformation (p. 160).

In our own work (Calabrese Barton & Tan, 2009), we have shown how a 6th-grade teacher and his students re-authored the multiple places of their classroom over the course of months in ways that pushed back against the oppressive structures experienced there. Located in a low-performing school in the heart of one of the nation's poorest congressional districts, the school had a history of low test scores. Most science instruction occurred in what youth referred to as a "drill and kill" format as their teacher sought his best to cover the tested materials. The school offered free breakfast and lunch to all students. However, many students stated they would rather "starve" than eat the school food, as eating school food held a social stigma despite its commonplace structure. Through youth and teacher codesigned lessons, the students engaged in learning activities that brought them out to local bodegas and into their homes, bringing in cultural repertoires of practice that positioned them as "local science experts" who not only taught one another science, but also shared "real" food to eat in science class and oral histories of their families' food and science experiences. The intersecting places of school science, neighborhood corner stores, local stories of food and the home, and the physical place of the classroom literally and figuratively transformed as youth re-created them in political, pedagogical, and physical ways.

Movement is an important way to draw attention to equity-related concerns. When youth make, they engage in the process of re-authoring and re-mixing practices from a wide range of experiences, located in the home, community, and school, among other places. As a form of multidisciplinary engagement, making manifests itself in how tools and practices from a wide domain of experiences (e.g., sewing and circuitry) are creatively brought together to create new things (e.g., e-textiles). Multi-practices can challenge normative views of STEM-rich making precisely because of how ideas, tools, and practice move and become remixed. For example, there are well-documented studies that show how "historically feminized" practices such as crafting take place alongside more traditionally "masculinized" practices such as electronics in powerful youth-based making (Buchholz, Shively, Peppler, & Wohlwend, 2014, p. 283). These ideals are echoed in Kafai et al.'s (2014) work, which shows how makerspaces bring together "hard" and "soft" skills toward challenging what counts as legitimate STEM-rich making.

Intersectional Geometries of Power

Intersectional geometries of power play a role in how learning as movement takes shape and for whom. For example, broader sociohistorical narratives around who can be a maker influence how youth come to a makerspace seeing themselves as capable in making. As we consider our work with youth from low-income communities of color in making spaces, we want to pay attention to how the shifting nature of STEM, making, and community places is always under negotiation, resulting in potential in-between spaces as different individuals reproduce and resist the narratives at play there. We are concerned, for example, with how unequal distributions of power take shape across the powered boundaries of gender, race, and class, impacting the making spaces the youth inhabit.

We use the phrase *intersectional geometries of power* to directly reference the importance of intersectional injustices in how maker learning plays out in the day-to-day experiences of young people—and the ways in which young people understand and respond to these injustices. As we referenced in Chapter 1, finding meaningful participation in making can be an ongoing struggle for individuals as they negotiate relationships between personal and historical narratives regarding participation with STEM-oriented making when these experiences differ from the norm (Holland & Lave, 2009).

The idea of intersectionality references the ways in which systemic oppressions play out in human interaction and activity (Crenshaw, 1991; Nash 2008). Intersectionality not only highlights the tangled webs of oppression, but also urges the formation of dynamic alliances toward social transformation, once these interconnecting webs can be named, identified, and understood (Nash, 2008; Unterhalter, 2012). We use this framing because we wish to push back against overstressing individual "uniqueness" without structural, power analysis (Rios, Bowling, & Harris, 2016).

Intersectional geometries of power delineate the complexity of systemic oppressive forces, while also calling attention to the social transformative goals underlying intersectional experiences. It calls our attention to how maker learning always draws strength from, as well as reflects, multiple perspectives, with differing experiences based on how one is positioned within matrices of power.

There is much attention placed on how the maker movement ought to support people in acting on their interests. But we caution that youth's interests are always reflections of their lived experiences in the world, and how they have learned to navigate those experiences through inter-sectional geometries of power. The cultural assets that youth from non-dominant communities bring to learning and engaging STEM are often perceived as deficit or are delegitimized by sociohistorical narratives and systemic practices of oppression (Calabrese Barton & Tan, 2010; Tzou, Scalone, & Bell, 2010). While young people experience these injustices at the local scale, they are driven by sociohistorical structures and narra-tives. The places of learning and doing STEM (including STEM-rich mak-ing spaces) are not particularly safe places for such youth. Comments of the youth—like Fall, whose blog post we shared at the start of the chapter—on wanting to feel safe and supported in making that helps to imagine new social futures are a strong pushback against these oppressive narratives. Their experiences can expose and challenge *normative views of making* while also building a making community that legitimizes their lives. However, how connections and interests are interpreted by others impacts determinations of who can make, and where making matters. This stance calls attention to equitable and consequential considerations of maker learning, for it foregrounds the ways in which individual experi-ences in making intersect with systemic forces through sanctioned power hierarchies and practices.

Place and Place-Making

The third part of this framework relates to the materials and social dimen-sions of place—as we consider the work youth do in makerspaces. We purposefully focus on *place* here rather than the term *space* more conven-tionally used in the "makerspace" movement. Place generally incorporates cultural connections and meanings through social, cultural, geographic, and political relationships and activities (Gruenwald & Smith, 2008). These connections are often not an elaborated dimension of space, which tends to be more abstract, without personal social connections (Tuan, 1977/2001). Though we will refer to maker*spaces*, or making *spaces*, when we invoke youth engaged *in meaningful activity with others in sociocultural context within them*, we will invoke the language of place. We wish to call attention to the ways in which *the place of making* is both relational and historicized (Rubel, Hall-Weickert, & Lim, 2017). Specifically, we take a critical geography per-spective on place, where place is made up of location (where), locale (the material settings for social relations that make up a place), and sense of place (subjective and emotional attachment) (Lombard, 2014). Here, we thus see place as a reflection of "a territory defined by practice-based learn-ing, inhabited by a network of people, ideas, and objects in movement" rather than a fixed geographical area (Fendler, 2013, p. 787).

Place-making is one way of making sense of the social construction of place (Lombard, 2014) across *scales of activity*. Drawing upon Jurow and Shea (2015), we view scales of activity as the "interrelations between practices, technologies and people" that imbue situated social action with meaning (p. 288). There are always multiple scales of activity operating at once, such as both "local" and "global" scales as well as "historical," "future-oriented," and "life history" scales (p. 288). Place-making, therefore, is a way of making sense of how people and the place transform one another socially and materially in-the-moment and over time (Jones & Evans, 2012). An individual's opportunities to be and to become are shaped by place. Places influence what people do in them. At the same time, who one is gives meaning to place: "Places do not have intrinsic meanings and essences . . . the meanings of place are created through practice" (Cresswell, 1996, p. 17).

People have embodied connections with the sociality and materiality of place (Jones & Evans, 2012), foregrounding its dynamic nature as well as the complexity of the social relations that make up places (Taylor, 2017). The reflexivity between people and place is important because it focuses on the importance of human agency in making place—a focus on "practice" and "place as it is performed by the people who use it" (Lombard, 2014, p. 15). People seek to re-create place in ways that transform the meaning of place (Lombard, 2013). Given our equity focus, we are particularly interested in these forms of critical agency (Green, 2015), making sense of how people "resist the construction of expectations about practices through place by using places and their established meanings in subversive ways" (Cresswell, 2014, p 27). Thus, we pay attention to how the possible platforms for being and becoming are not only solely contingent on the structural landscape of geographical places but also tied to norms and power structures (Rubel et al., 2017).

Place-making is also important because it calls attention to the agency that people have, both individually and collectively, to construct place in ongoing ways (Green, 2015). Such action, however, is always entangled with issues of power supported by the material and social structures of place. For example, in a study of hand-pulled rickshaws in Calcutta, Hyrapiet and Greiner (2012) show how rickshaw pullers (wallahs) engage in a wide range of interactions and services that extend beyond the traditional practice of pulling rickshaws. Pullers sleep at doorsteps to provide security. They make tactical decisions to avoid police raids. They also establish impromptu rickshaw stands in unconventional places. These extended practices allow pullers to embed themselves in place in ways that make them "indispensable," challenging "power geometries" of "who belongs where" (p. 420). As Hyrapiet and Greiner (2012) further explain: "Much of the work the rickshaw wallahs perform constitutes a kind of 'place making' that enmeshes them in the routines of daily life and from which they have generated considerable social capital" (p. 419).

What is of interest to us in a Mobilities of Criticality framework are the ways in which place-making is deeply connected to movement and power: The movement of ideas, resources, practices, and so forth produce tensions and contradictions, especially as young people seek to enact agency within contexts of oppression or marginalization. From this perspective, place-making is an often-contested process. Any given individual's experience in a place produces different meanings and value because of how one is positioned within the material settings and social relations of place (Massey, 2005). As Friedmann (2007) illustrates in his study of place-making and "place-breaking" in urban China, places are shaped by the everyday lives of the visible *and* invisible policies and practices of the state or dominant structures. This stance on movement raises questions about the ways in which maker learning is always under negotiation as different individuals reproduce and resist the narratives at play in their places of making.

Presence — seeing struggle as legitimate presence & borders alone do not constitute belonging

The insights above emphasize the creative elements of human action and interaction, which are fundamental to reconstructing place as locations, but also as sites of meaning-making. From an equity in making standpoint, this is significant as we consider how policies and practices of dominant culture shape the place of STEM-rich making, and the ways in which the construction of places by people and actions can be delegitimized through the ongoing stereotyping of specific types of place through dominant processes of knowledge production.

An important dimension of place-making we believe to be that of "a rightful presence" in place. Rightful presence, an idea that has emerged from critical justice studies of borderland and refugee communities in welcoming host countries, captures the ongoing social and political struggles for legitimacy by guests in these host settings (Barnett, 2005). Rightful presence challenges the normative guest/host relationships by critiquing the limitations of framing a welcome to place through the "extension" of a static set of rights to newcomers (Squire, 2009). Instead, rightful presence calls for the disruption of normative power relations, reconfiguring what it means to legitimately belong in a place (Squire, 2009). Legitimately belonging means more than having the borders of practice opened to new comers (e.g., expanding who has a right to participate within community). It means understanding and seeing moments of social and political struggle as forms of legitimate presence.

Enacting rightful presence is both dynamic and contentious. Moments of struggle are always an ongoing reflection of the historicized injustices outsiders have encountered in relation to participation in community. In a study of "citizenship," Vrasti and Dayal (2016) illustrate how even when sanctuary city nondiscriminatory mandates legislate access to public commons and services, "atmospheric walls" (immaterial walls with material effects) of "whiteness, masculinity, and class privilege" mediate access in practice (p. 994). However, local practices grounded in minor political reactions to majority legitimized activity can "facilitate movements and exchanges that were not there before," opening up moments (existing both in a time and place) of possible rightful presence (p. 999). Here, we see how injustices are always in-action as they take shape through institutionalized practices and mandates as well as through power-driven sociocultural norms.

HOW WE USE A MOBILITIES OF CRITICALITY FRAMEWORK

From an equity standpoint, a Mobilities of Criticality framework offers important conceptual tools for studying maker learning in community settings (see Table 2.1). First, this framing provides ways to make sense of how youth participate in making practices within community in ways that challenge normative views, such as by making visible how their work challenges normative boundaries (e.g., formal/informal, novice/expert, and past, present, and future), and how these boundaries change over time and across space (Rahm, 2014). From this perspective, we are interested in how new routines, ideas, and ways of being become legitimized in practice.

Additionally, this framework provides ways to make sense of how learning and doing are situated within local culture, but also contribute to that culture. How actors are positioned (and by whom) across time and space for what they bring to making all shape opportunities to learn and become (Bang & Medin, 2010). Unequal distribution of power impacts whether or not one sees oneself as capable and welcomed in STEM (Nasir, 2011), often resulting in youth losing interest in STEM before high school. Thus, to understand maker learning in-practice requires one to pay attention to the power dynamics that shape how youth are recognized for what they know and can do. Holland and Lave (2001) argue, "in practice, material and symbolic resources are distributed disproportionally across socially identified groups and generate different social relations and perspectives among participants in such groups" (p. 5). As individuals join new communities of practice, such as making spaces, they call upon salient practices and ways of being that are learned in that community, as well as from other places. These actions can position individuals as either central or marginal to their new community depending upon how they are received by others. These unequal distributions of power can impact whether or not one sees oneself as capable and welcomed in STEM or in making (Vossoughi et al., 2016).

Lastly, this framework provides conceptual approaches for making sense of how youth's making present practices are always in dialectic with the past and present, but directionally enacted toward current and future social change making. Attending to scales of activity across time and place matters in the youth's making efforts. One aspect that is especially important here is attention to the risks and tensions youth makers may

Table 2.1. Mobilities of Criticality

	Key Ideas	Implications for Maker Learning
Movement	Ideas, norms, and practices move with people as bodies move through spaces, impacting established norms of spaces	How to be open to youth-empowering ideas and concerns that they bring to the making space; how to recognize and minimize negative norms from larger spaces that might constrain youth makers
Intersectional Geometries of Power	Salient youth identities, relationality, and concerns from their everyday life, against a historicized background; historicized backgrounds of communities	Who youth are and want to be is tied to their histories involving systemic and intersecting injustices—how does this factor into what kinds of artifacts get made, and through what kinds of processes?
Place and Place-making	Through enacting practices, people can mark places with specific meanings, sometimes new Place-making is contentious	What kinds of support, pedagogical or otherwise, can help youth makers start to place-make and author a rightful presence in making? What kinds of new practices would youth makers seed to build an empowering community maker culture?
Presence	Gaining authentic legitimacy in a place/system in ways that do not require denying of one's salient ways of being	How do we know when youth have successfully authored a rightful presence?

face as their work pushes up against the intersectional power geometries of their places of making.

MOBILITIES OF CRITICALITY: WHY WE FOCUS OUR WORK IN COMMUNITY PARTNERSHIPS

Community-Centered Making Space Partnerships

Our study is grounded in middle-school youth's experiences in two community-centered making space programs in Michigan and North Carolina, over the course of 4 years. The MI maker program has been active since 2007; however, it has slowly taken a more direct focus in "making" from a more general focus on "engineering" since 2013. NC's maker program began in 2014 with an explicit making focus. The making space programs are housed in "Youth Clubs," which are community-based clubs serving low-income families, with a focus on youth development, homework help, and sports for youth from low-income backgrounds. Both clubs serve predominantly (> 95%) multigenerational African American communities alongside much smaller percentages of White and Latinx youth.

We partnered with these institutions because they: (1) centralize equity in STEM in their programs, (2) offer programs that promote sustained experiences in making, and (3) recruit a diversity of youth (e.g., ages, ethnicity, SES, gender) into making, including homeless youth, youth of color, and low-income youth.

An open-door policy was held in both sites for the making programs. Youth were recruited by club directors for a variety of reasons—an interest in STEM, a need to keep a youth occupied, and friendship groups. These were not drop-in programs, but sustained after-school programs. Youth participated in weekly making sessions for a full school year, with many participating for 2 or more years. Given the nature of youth lives, many moved in and out of these programs as their lives allowed (e.g., some youth faced transient housing situations, had transportation issues, or had arts or competitive sports seasons at school). For example, Samuel, the student whose story is presented in Chapter 1, once missed 2 months of programming because he lacked transportation to his club. In most cases, the youth who left the programs completely were the ones who moved away from the area or stopped their participation at the Youth Club for reasons often beyond their control.

In our research and development roles, we worked collaboratively with Youth Club staff to establish making programs over time, with the goal of supporting youth in learning about STEM-rich making in culturally sustaining ways. We sought to engage youth iteratively and generatively in making activities by incorporating youth-led community ethnography (discussed in more detail in Chapter 4). We conjectured that a community ethnography approach to making might provide a way to support youth in moving and embedding local knowledge, practice, and wisdom more explicitly into making in ways that both legitimize local knowledge as powerful within STEM, but which also restructured the knowledge/practice hierarchies there. While we codesigned activities with this main conjecture in mind, we did not know how this approach would work in particular, or the implications it had for what, how, or why youth might make, since community-insider data would reside primarily with the youth and not with us. For example, when youth decided they were interested in safety concerns, we worked with them to design an open-ended survey they could give to community members to solicit their experiences and ideas about safety, but youth had input into who they wanted to survey.

We have been particularly interested in community-centered making, and this is the primary reason we sought to work with our partners. In this study, *community-centered* carried *three* interrelated meanings, tied to our Mobilities of Criticality framework. First, the making spaces were housed in community centers and followed norms for participation reflective of those community spaces. For example, programs were inter-age (generally ages 10–15), supported flexible movement in and out of programs due to transient life circumstances while also promoting sustained engagement (as explained above), and involved youth in ongoing codesign of experiences.

Second, the two focal making programs sought to create spaces for youth to interact with the broader community served by the youth clubs. While the design of the experiences was meant to support youth in engaging with their communities in making, we did not know how this would play out beyond our design ideas, and we expected our design ideas to be transformed by these experiences. For example, early on in the making process, youth were encouraged to interview community members and peers on pertinent issues that they thought they could address through making practices. Community members were sought out by the youth because of existing relationships youth had. This involved an organic approach of extending the net of relations that individuals within the space had. Taking such community funds of knowledge as their initial research sources, youth moved through iterative making design cycles of further online and community ethnographic research, making/prototyping/testing at their making spaces, with critical feedback sessions with community experts.

As part of refining the problems youth decided to solve, making space educators encouraged youth to engage with community dialogue through ongoing observations, surveys, and informal conversations to learn more about the challenges/problems that community members faced and the kinds of advice/ideas they had for solving those problems. Youth were encouraged to talk with peers at school, club, and around their neighborhood. They were also guided to conduct open-ended surveys of their parents, friends' parents, and other youth and adults around their club, schools, and neighborhood. They were supported in identifying and systematically observing locations and contexts of safety concerns as timing and safety allowed (e.g., observing a playground where bullying occurred with help from adults). Each week, making space educators helped youth to analyze their stories, interactions, and other data they collected, discussing patterns and exploring standout ideas together as learning partners.

Third, making space educators periodically designed activities or events that brought community members into the community center to provide feedback or help on projects. For example, youth participated in multiple feedback cycles with different community constituents, and coordinated these feedback sessions with different points in their making design cycle, to solicit the types of technical and/or social input that could help them move their design work forward. This sometimes took on a more formal tone as youth presented their projects to various stakeholders (e.g., local engineers, parents, community members, and peers) who provided written feedback, or when youth involved various community members as prototype testers. Sometimes these feedback cycles were more informal, as various community members visited youth at their workstations and engaged in idea-generating conversations.

A Note on Research Methodology: Critical Ethnography as Complementary to a Mobilities of Criticality Framework

desire-based framework [handwritten margin note]

Being critically engaged with equity in making methodological decisions, we have been concerned with how we lens our work, giving privilege to the youth with whom we work—youth whose voices have been absent in the formalization of the maker movement. We follow an unapologetic assets-driven and "desire-based" framework (in refusal of "damage-centered research" [Tuck, 2009], which has for too long positioned youth from nondominant communities as in need of repair, a strong narrative in STEM education).

We thus carried out our study as a critical ethnography over a 4-year period. Critical ethnography was selected because of its explicit focus on participatory critique, transformation, empowerment, and social justice. We are also concerned with understanding the cultural dimensions of making programs and youth's participation. Critical ethnography is well suited to help us make sense of the cultural dimensions of making while also foregrounding and making sense of inequalities from multiple perspectives (Trueba, 1999). Ethnography places an emphasis on understanding *cultural systems*. We are interested in generating understandings of the dynamic STEM-making culture in each of the two sites through representation of emic perspectives, or the insider's point of view (Erickson, 1984). We were also interested in a long-term, holistic view of the programs under study, to generate a rich and dynamic portrait of the cultural systems at play, how they develop over time in interaction with individuals, tools, resources, and experience, and how the youth themselves learn and become as makers through this culture. This is a time- and labor-intensive research approach, but given the new and changing nature of the maker movement, we felt that conducting these longitudinal ethnographies was essential.

Critical ethnography also provided an approach with which to "politicize" the interaction between actors and the social structures through which they act, grounded in the belief that these relationships are never neutral. That is, we work to see how culture and power play out in human action and interaction, keeping problematic the ways in which dominant narratives can frame what it means to know, do, and become in these spaces. This approach was important as we attempted to make sense of how youth, who are positioned in particular ways due to race, gender, and class, engage in making space activities.

Our multiyear focus has allowed us to follow youth through multiple making projects, as well to deepen the kinds of trusted relationships required for the depth of insight needed in ethnographic work. We do not believe that we could have documented the emerging culture of making if we had been present only for 1 year, or even if we had dropped in and out over time. Embedding ourselves longitudinally allowed us to establish legitimate presence in the communities, which is essential to our efforts to identify how youth's making practices emerge, develop, and move through space and time.

Study used ethnographies as a way to examine the inequalities from multiple perspectives

LOOKING AHEAD

Power dynamics are always at play in making as they are also in STEM-related domains, whether these power dynamics are explicitly acknowledged or not. This is fundamentally an equity concern for youth from nondominant communities whose cultural knowledge and practice has historically been marginal to school and disciplinary knowledge and practices.

Youth historically marginalized in both STEM and the maker movement, even if positioned as a welcomed guest in a makerspace (which is not always the case), are often expected to reconfigure themselves toward the majority culture. As such, their participation is subject to an uneven power dynamic where their welcomedness could be undone at any moment. Such perilous positioning is related to the intersection of youth's identities (and identity markers) in other areas of their lives, as youth of color, as a particular gender, as an African American, as a youth from a low-income background. A Mobilities of Criticality framework can help us understand the different ways in which youth are positioned as lesser across these areas of their lived experiences, and how such unjust experiences intersect and move across spaces and time to impact local experiences and practices when youth are engaged in community making.

CHAPTER 3

"We Want a Makerspace!"
Youth Participatory Action Research Toward the Design of Equity-Oriented Making

with Myungwhan Shin, Christina Restrepo Nazar,
Day Greenberg, and 16 Youth Makers

> I try to do things outside of school that let me explore my interests like making things. . . . I am naturally an inventor. I make things out of anything . . . pretty much if you tell me what you want, I can most likely make it. Like something so small can become something so big. My first experience making something came when I was in elementary school. I actually did it because of many reasons, like I liked making things, but it was also because I needed to. —Alie, 14 years old

Alie is a prolific maker. She participated in a maker club at her community center, and further worked extensively at home on duct tape and lotion products for her family and peers as gifts and through special orders. She told us that she uses her making to help people. She understands the challenges of growing up without many resources, and wants to use those experiences to help her reach others: "I have always had a passion for helping people. . . . I love giving back to the community. I remember where I come from, and I remember how it used to be, and remember the struggle."

On her "duct tape evolution" website, Alie provides pictures of a wide range of products, including duct tape hats with reversible designs, duct tape flowers of different colors to stick on pens or pencils, a duct tape mannequin made from an "old T-shirt that is my size, stuffed with plastic bags with duct tape over it for support." She describes that she uses her mannequin "to sew back together my clothes when they rip or when I want to make a new design from old T-shirts." Not only does Alie want people to have the things they need and may not be able to afford, but she believes that people should be "allowed to have colorful things at work and in school, and express who they truly are."

Alie is thoughtfully and critically aware of the ways in which making can be consequential to her life and to the lives of the people she cares about. She has sought to blend her fashion sense with STEM-rich approaches to produce new tools that she feels are needed by those she cares for. Alie, who lives with her dad, over several months in her maker club created a solar-powered thermometer system within a fashionable duct tape tie. She felt it could help her dad, and others who may be ill, to have ongoing awareness of their body's temperature, without having to worry about being awakened every hour to have their temperature taken, or worry about the hygiene of oral thermometers. Tech-rich knowledge of circuitry, renewable energy, and materials, combined with health concerns, knowledge of fashionable and affordable ties, and hospital routines all mattered in her making work.

At the same time, Alie is cognizant of how her efforts are supported—or not—by the places where she lives and learns. To Alie, school is a place where her making is not supported because "In school we learn things and then we do tests on what we learn and then we move on. We really don't have time to see what we're interested in. I try to do things outside of school that let me explore my interests like making things." At the same time, she limits her duct tape work to either her community club or home because these are places where she feels "welcomed," "wanted," and "safe." She wants to make in ways that allow her to continue to be who she is, and to make from that vantage point as a powerful strength, or in her words, "a super power." She writes on her website that her after-school club

> is very different from our regular science classroom because there is more free will in what we can do and how our inventions affect our communities and who they are for and what purpose. I am showing you this website and my designs in hopes that you see how we can help people with the ways we are, like the evolution of our history, because that's how we learn to be who we are.

Alie's story gives credence to the mantra "Anyone can make, anywhere." Her story, however, cautions us to be mindful of whose voices and experiences have helped shape this new making culture, and how that plays out in the kinds of makerspace programs and designs that youth have access to. Who youth are and want to be in making—especially youth growing up in nondominant communities—has not been central to the maker movement, especially as it relates to the design of making spaces. The maker movement offers an egalitarian ideal; however, participation in making may only become equitable when the spaces, the experiences, and the pedagogies-in-practice recognize, support, and value the potentially full and complex lives that youth bring to making.

What do youth want out of their making spaces and why? How do youth make a place for themselves while participating in making? If we reflect on Alie's ideas, we see that she is arguing for a kind of place where she has a rightful presence in STEM-rich making. She wants to be accepted and supported for who she is—her history, needs, desires, and potential future. And, she wants to leverage that as a place of strength for her making. Her words and actions inscribe new meanings for what it means to make within the places she inhabits, refiguring participation in these places and their possibilities for her learning and becoming within them. But how such places of making are made themselves, over time, and in interactions with others and place, has not been a central focus of the maker movement. In this chapter, we examine one group of youth's efforts to author making places where they have a rightful presence, through an intensive Youth Participatory Action Research (YPAR) project.

DESIGN OF MAKING ENVIRONMENTS

There is much written in the research literature and popular media on the design of makerspaces and how physical designs relate to the kinds of making made possible (Maker Media, 2013; Peppler, Halverson, & Kafai, 2016; Sheridan et al., 2014). As Maker Media (2013) reminds us, "Makerspaces come in all shapes and sizes, but they all serve as a gathering point for tools, projects, mentors and expertise" (p. 1). Indeed, Maker Media (2013), with the publication of their *Makerspace Playbook*, has led the field in thinking about critical design features in support of 21st-century making. While they note that making happens everywhere, from the high-tech fablab to the kitchen table, design considerations for makerspaces are critical in making a "real difference in how enthusiastic and successful students are in making and achieving their project visions" (p. 5).

From an educational research standpoint, the design of makerspaces has received increasing attention because maker learning cannot be separated from the maker contexts in which learners participate or the possibilities for maker learning (Peppler et al., 2016). Making is learner-driven and inquiry-oriented, where makers are positioned as creative producers of ideas and things rather than consumers of knowledge and technologies (Maker Media, 2013). Makers need opportunities for structured learning and skill development, project-based work, and creative playfulness.

Though there is much that is written about the variety of tools and their applications in making, we are interested in the principles that undergird the design of making places—the principles that play out in designs that contribute to who one is and can be in a making place. We are particularly concerned with those guiding principles that speak more broadly to equity in making. From this vantage point, two key design principles widely touted and agreed upon broadly in the field include the *key design principles* [handwritten annotation]

need for (a) transparency and accessibility, and (b) mobility and flexibility (Halverson & Sheridan, 2014).

Transparency and accessibility refer to the importance of participants being able to see and use the materials, tools, and ideas housed within a makerspace. Design features such as transparent walls or adequate openings/windows promote a sense of openness and allow people to see what is happening inside the space and to feel that they may be welcome inside. Transparent storage bins or open-access pegboards for tool storage, all within reach, also promote access. Mobility and flexibility refer to designing the makerspace so that resources can move with users in ways that users need in the moment. For example, furniture (tables and chairs) and storage bins should be mobile to allow for groups to organically form and dissolve. Space organized by theme or area of work (e.g., sewing/crafting area, laser cutter area, robotics area) makes particular making skills more obvious and easier to access; at the same time, it is suggested that these areas be expandable and collapsible depending upon the day or activity.

Although the design-focused literature in making addresses makerspaces broadly, there is a small but growing body of literature that focuses specifically on the design of youth-oriented makerspaces. For example, Keune, Gomoll, and Peppler (2015) have studied how the physical artifacts of a making space can promote making opportunities for young people that are pliable (invitation to change and shape artifacts), mobile (potential to physically move artifacts in a space), and accessible (transparency and availability of artifacts to all). The authors argue that these qualities are important because learning happens as the individual and the surrounding physical and social environment interact.

For example, the presence of a handwritten community schedule "made of cardboard and suspended from a thumbtack" that lists activities and times and hangs visibly from the entry way suggests to those present that "anyone" could make or edit the schedule for the makerspace. In another example, the authors show how hanging artifacts completed by youth and made of inexpensive materials (e.g., cardboard) throughout the makerspace, with signage illustrating their collaborative construction, increased the pliability and accessibility of making for others who viewed or interacted with these artifacts.

how do we meet key design principles in low-income communities? [handwritten annotation]

There are fewer studies, however, that address the design of makerspaces in low-income communities, where the financial burdens for acquiring tools and space for building makerspaces can be significantly limited. Sheridan et al. (2014) tackle this concern directly, with their examination of the design of the Mt. Elliott makerspace located in a church basement in Detroit. Mt. Elliott was designed to be both "a model for makerspaces that can thrive in under-resourced neighborhoods by minimizing expenses and ensuring no financial barriers to participation" (p. 516).

Being located in a church basement is significant. With open hours on Sundays and 2 days after school, church members are free to participate in activities after services, and parents may feel more comfortable having their children there after school. Furthermore, because the director is the only paid staff member, experienced participants take on impromptu teaching roles in these spaces as newcomers join the space. The authors further note that the space is made up of several rooms, including rooms or areas for woodworking, electronics, silk-screening, and digital fabrication. They describe how the space is continually evolving, "with different shops added over time as interest in or [as] resources for new activities emerge" (p. 516). Of these separate but connected spaces, the authors state that they "support focused work in a given area while also encouraging community connections and flow among the making disciplines" (p. 516).

In another publication, Sheridan and Konopasky (2016) argue for the importance of an "ethos of resourcefulness" as a key design feature of this same making space. According to these authors, an ethos of resourcefulness, a "stance to use what you have and persist and innovate to meet needs and wants—is a more critical part of a community-based makerspace than any particular activity or learning" (p. 30). The idea of designing for resourcefulness means that the physical space itself supports youth in working individually or in groups on self-directed projects or playful activities through an open and flexible design where "all activities are visible in the entire space" and where the physical space has furniture that allows for on-site and changing partnerships. An important aspect of this is "tools and materials organized, accessible and labeled" and physical structures that can transform, for example, movable furniture, writable tables, and walls, and digital tools allowing for shared documents. All of these design features push back against the layers of access because of what one knows or one's familiarity with tools. For example, the design feature of "open shop," made possible by the transparent access to tools and materials, allows participants the opportunity to work on what they want and seek the kind of help they want. Visible mission statements make explicit that participants are encouraged to share their ideas, skills, ideas, materials, and/or tools as a part of building up "the community's resources" (p. 45). This harkens back to the design research on access and opportunity in adult-based makerspaces where tools and materials are stored in transparent bins or hung on walls, allowing for visibility and ease of access (Keune et al., 2015).

Powerful as this design work has been, most design work of makerspaces has been produced by adults, who themselves may be outsiders to communities. Little of the design-based work on making spaces has taken a decidedly *youth-centered* point of view. These design features alone may not fully attend to some of the structural inequalities enhanced by the making movement, such as what it means to be a youth maker, or what kinds of activities, ways of being, or ideas and products produced are valued in a making space.

Adults are [~~not~~] designing makerspaces but maybe + should be youth designed *[handwritten annotation:]* – Research w/ to identify Youth problems in makerspaces designs

YOUTH PARTICIPATORY ACTION RESEARCH

We took a Youth Participatory Action Research (YPAR) to the design of making spaces because we sought to challenge traditional ideas of who has the authority to produce knowledge and whose knowledge is deemed valuable in social science (Bautista, Bertrand, Morrell, Scorza, & Matthews, 2013; Cammarota & Fine, 2008; Fine, 2008). By deliberately inverting who frames the problem, who constructs research designs, and who interprets the findings, YPAR empowers youth who have been historically excluded or oppressed to deconstruct the deficient views, oppressive systems, and subjugating discourses affecting their daily lives (Bautista et al., 2013; Fine, 2008). Knowledge generated from YPAR is always co-constructed toward activist ends. In other words, we hoped to use the findings from YPAR as launching pads for actions to initiate social change rather than as mere facts stored in academic literature (Cammarota & Fine, 2008; Morrell, 2006). Here, we see youth's insights as "a critical epistemology that redefines knowledge as actions in pursuit of social justice" (Cammarota & Fine, 2008, p. 6).

This approach mattered to us because we sought to position youth as active partners in the research process whose perspectives, experiences, and expertise in the world matter to the research agenda. Throughout YPAR, we conducted research *with* the youth, rather than *on* the youth (Rodríguez & Brown, 2009; Sato, 2013). As coresearchers, youth were positioned to identify the problems in makerspace design that mattered to them, and to design the investigations, interpret data, and identify action to be taken to transform what they felt might be unjust. This required a collaborative process and mutual beneficial relationships; the authority during the research process is shared between the adult and the youth researchers (Duncan-Andrade & Morrell, 2008). Furthermore, our YPAR approach was grounded in the belief that the youth—who historically have been marginalized in the maker movement, especially STEM-rich making—were uniquely positioned to "reveal wisdom about the history, structure, consequences, and the fracture points in unjust social arrangement" (Fine, 2008, p. 215). Through this process, the youth's voices, lived experiences, and histories could become legitimate intellectual resources in YPAR projects (Morrell, 2006).

THE UNFOLDING OF AN INVESTIGATION

In our efforts to cocreate an authentic, community-based making space, we collaborated with 16 youth at one of our partner sites to conduct a YPAR project on makerspace design. Thirteen of the youth were African American girls (9) and boys (4), and three were White girls. They were mainly from grades 6–10 (ages 11–16). Most of them regularly attended a maker program at their local community club. The main goal of the project was to design a new youth-centered makerspace in a local after-school club to challenge the traditional design/notion of maker-spaces that may shape the participation of youth from lower-income communities of color.

During the previous 3 school years, the youth at their community club participated in their maker program in the club's all-purpose room, used also as a cafeteria, a dance classroom, and a tae kwon do classroom (among other uses), often simultaneously. Consequently, while the program was not in session, the youth had to store their projects along with the few tools and machines we had, such as laptops, a sewing machine, and hand tools, in a locked file cabinet or place them in the main office area so that the other programs could fully use the space.

Although the youth seemed to enjoy their maker club, they also wanted to improve it. They wanted to be able to have greater access to their projects throughout the week, whether to work on them or to show them to others. They also wanted a place where they would have fewer distractions and more space to work. However, the center had limited space and a tight budget. When the youth had maker club programs after school, other community center youth ate snacks at tables next to their club, separated only by an accordion-style divider. The youth who were making in the makerspace were often disturbed by noise from the cafeteria, and vice versa. Often, many of the youth makers would move into the main office area when working on digital fabrications to reduce background noise, but this space was not always openly available.

During the summer of 2015, we sought to host a maker camp for the youth on our university campus. We felt that it would provide youth with time away from the hubbub of the club, and would give us a chance to let the youth visit other real-world makerspaces on campus. The goal of the summer experience was to provide more sustained opportunities to make, while also supporting the youth in developing concrete ideas on how we could improve our space back at the club.

We began the week by spending time investigating makerspaces in other cities through virtual tours, including the Mt. Elliott space discussed earlier in the chapter. Using the pictures and videos of the makerspaces posted on makerspace websites, the youth explored the design features of the makerspaces. Through their virtual tours, the youth were able to see what makerspaces in other cities looked like, and were able to practice data collection methods before physically visiting makerspaces in their community.

This led to dialogue with the youth about what they valued in these spaces, and what they wanted to learn by visiting other makerspaces. For example, some of the youth commented on how they liked the fact that Mt. Elliott's website included videos that showed people working on projects, and also that it was located in a church rather than a school. They also liked that there seemed to be many different kinds of projects that one could work on, but they were concerned that taking over the whole basement of a church was not realistic for them, as their community club did not even have a basement.

Based on the discussions, we codesigned observation protocols that helped the youth systematically collect data. For example, one of the protocols involved the youth recording design features of the makerspaces that made them feel safe, welcomed, and/or engaged. These criteria were their terms that they felt mattered to them in making. The youth also designed a protocol that included interview questions for the makerspace staff or makers (e.g., What do you do here? What do you like best about this place? What would you change about this place if you could?), with a space for their answers to the questions.

After designing protocols, the youth split up into four teams to facilitate their data collection. Each group member had specific roles for the investigations, such as the interviewer, the photographer, and the notetaker.

Then they visited three area makerspaces in person, two at a local university campus and one at a local science center. During the visits, the youth examined the design features of the makerspaces, such as the layout, tools, equipment, and atmosphere (Figure 3.1). In particular, they studied what made them feel safe and what was engaging or welcoming about these features. They also interviewed the staff or managers of the makerspaces using the list of questions in the worksheets they designed. Using iPads, portable cameras, and worksheets, the youth collaboratively collected the data.

After visiting these spaces, the youth conducted research at their own community club. They interviewed peers, parents, and staff members for their views and feelings about STEM and about making. They measured different spaces in the club to develop a plan for where they might house a more permanent making space. For example, to acquire accurate measurements of dimensions for sketching a new makerspace, the youth first measured the dimensions of the room in which their makerspace was originally placed. They then investigated other rooms and areas at their club, and explored possible options for a new making space.

CRITICAL MOMENTS

What unfolded throughout the YPAR was not what we had envisioned, though we take that as a strength, as it means it was truly led by youth insights. By the end of the first set of investigations of campus makerspaces, the youth had expressed deep concern that the making spaces on campus

Figure 3.1. Sketch of Makerspace

they visited were "not for us"—they felt uncomfortable and unwelcomed in those spaces. It was not that the makerspace staff did not welcome the youth to their spaces. They did, and generously offered their time to show the youth about and answer all of their questions. Rather, as they indicated in their comments, the youth were unsure that they could make—or be—in ways they wished.

In what follows we describe four key moments of the YPAR and what they meant: (1) A Kid-friendly Space: Unraveling Power Dynamics, (2) Taking a Stance: "Our Club Makerspace Manifesto," (3) designing a workshop on "Teach, Show, Design, and Make" and (4) conducting the workshop at a meeting of the board of directors of the community club.

A Kid-Friendly Space: Unraveling Power Dynamics

During the first debriefing session, we focused on making sense of the observations and interviews the youth conducted. The conversation started off slowly until Ivy exclaimed with some degree of exasperation, "I didn't realize that most makerspaces are really *just not for kids. We have a different view.*" This led to animated dialogue, as they built on one another's ideas to flesh out this concern:

Caitlyn: It was a *grown-up* makerspace; it wasn't colorful.

Day [Mentor, who is recording ideas on a shared Google Doc projected
   on the screen]: Grown-up makerspace, wasn't colorful.

[Everyone starts talking at once; Day calls on Patricia]

Patricia: It was serious.

Day: Serious.

Patricia: There was barely any space!

Day: Not enough space. Ivy, what did you say?

Ivy: There weren't any games.

Ashlee: There were too many people.

Patricia: There weren't fun enough experiments.

Mary: It didn't make you feel *welcomed.*

Patricia: It made you feel boring, it's boring. A kid makerspace would
   be colorful, you'd do fun experiments; you'd do serious but fun
   experiments.

Mary: I thought there'd be stuff like laid out for you to do.

Quentin: There was a lot of space but it wasn't open.

[handwritten margin note: most makerspaces are not kid-friendly (colorful, open, fun, experiments)]

This contrast noted by the youth—of "youth-friendly" versus
"adult-friendly"—emerged strongly in their conversations about their observations, and became an important point of contention. In the transcript
above, Caitlyn proclaims that "it was a *grown-up* makerspace," and Mary
says she did not feel "*welcomed.*" The youth were frustrated, and their observations emerged as *critiques* of the makerspaces they visited. We did not
anticipate this critique. We expected that their trips to the other makerspaces would spark interest in ideas they had for their space, not critiques of
these other spaces. However, we began to see the youth's dialogue showing
attention to concern about power dynamics in terms of (a) *what* they were
allowed to do ("no games," no "experiments") and (b) what they *felt* in
these spaces ("boring," "not colorful," "not welcomed," and "crowded."),
and (c) who they could be in these spaces ("grown-up" and "serious").

We sought to flip the question around to have the youth use their
critiques to point toward design elements of makerspaces that they *wanted
to see* in place that might attend to these concerns:

Angie [mentor]: Can I go back to a comment someone made a minute
   ago? I was really intrigued by the comment that "there wasn't
   enough stuff laid out and even if there was stuff out there, you
   didn't have good ideas [for how to use it]." So what does that
   mean to you? What would you like to see then?

The conversation that ensued, while raising ideas of things they
wanted to see (e.g., Ashlee: "More wires!," Mary: "Inspiration," Samuel:
"Small storage spaces," Rayna: "Working stations"), continued to focus on

their critique, this time with more direct focus on how the space marginalized youth. In the transcript segment below, Patricia was frustrated that they could not touch the equipment:

> *Patricia:* I heard the word *no* because you guys said we couldn't touch that board cutter and—
> *Day:* So there was stuff you weren't allowed to touch?
> *Patricia:* Yes. I want to be able to touch *everything*.
> *Day:* Okay, you want to be able to touch *everything*.
> *Patricia:* They should have put stuff out for us to do. I didn't want to just sit there and be looking at it like—
> *Day:* You don't want to sit there and be looking at it. I like that.
> *Patricia:* Sit there and look at it, not be looking at it.

In fact, in all 13 sets of youth-authored notes from the initial investigations, all the youth consistently noted that the spaces they visited were not colorful and did not have tools kids could access because they were too high or locked up. When tools were present, there were no visible instructions on how to use the things that were there.

At the same time, as mentors, we noticed that some of the ideas the youth were raising were not really captured in the initial observation and interview criteria. And so we decided to reorient the interviews and observation criteria before conducting further investigations.

> *Angie:* So I am wondering, you know we're going to another makerspace tomorrow, and I'm wondering is there anything from this conversation right now that gives you ideas about different questions you want to ask the person who's in charge? Like one question that comes to my mind from our conversation is "Do you actually take more stuff out when people are here?"
> *Ashlee:* Yeah!
> *Angie:* Now that you've had the experience of being in a makerspace, you have to be a little bit more informed about what you want to look for, what other things you might ask.
> *Samuel:* What invention would you make to save the world if you could? I asked Scott [an engineer] that, but I forgot to write it down.
> *Katana* [to Annabeth]: Did you come up with a question?
> *Annabeth:* Yup.
> *Katana:* What's your question?
> *Annabeth:* How many people are usually in your makerspace at a time?
> *Katana:* Oh, that's an interesting question! [To Rayna] Do you have a question?

[handwritten margin note:] tools that are kid-friendly or post directions on how to use certain tools

[Rayna nods her head yes]
Katana: What's your question?
Rayna: My question is, "What should I have for a question?"
Day [mentor]: Oh you could really be asking people, "What should I be asking you?"
Caitlyn: How about "What kind of things have been invented here?"

What seemed particularly interesting in this exchange was how the questions the young people came up with focused on their uniquely youth-centered and community-oriented ideas about making. Samuel's question, "What invention would you make to save the world if you could?" was later adapted by the youth to include a second and third follow-on question: "Does the makerspace have what you need to make that invention?" "What kinds of tools would you add?" These follow-on questions cemented their stance that making *ought to be for something.*

That the youth also cared about the things that they could not touch or see, further pushed to the fore the power dynamics they were implicitly critiquing. Rayna suggested three questions along these lines:

"What is there that I cannot see?"
"What questions should I be asking [that I have not asked]?"
"What would you change if you could?"

Thus, in these initial observations of makerspaces, the youth began to articulate a critique of the maker movement as positioning them as *outsiders.* This initial critique was focused primarily on how they felt as youth—unable to access tools because of their height or because they were not allowed, finding the spaces drab and boring and as places that lacked a sense of playfulness.

A second critique began to emerge through the interviews, largely around the purpose of the space, and this was evident in both Samuel's and Rayna's question contributions: Why do we make, and does the makerspace let us act on our concerns? In the next section, we see how youth began to merge these concerns together as they articulated their vision for a makerspace.

Taking a Stance: Authoring Makerspace Movies and Manifesto

Makerspace movies. On the third day of our camp, as teacher-researchers in this YPAR, we found that we had to regroup, and offer possible new directions the youth might take with their work that drew upon their important insights. We decided to task the youth to make short digital movies that communicated what they thought were the most important ideas from their findings. They were given wide berth in this task. They had only three requirements: The movies should (a) be no longer than 3–5 minutes, (b) explain to others what a makerspace is, and (c) use at least four different pieces of evidence from their investigations. They were given free rein on how to make the movie. Some groups used iMovie to cull together images, text, and music to present their ideas, while others combined iMovie and Photo Booth to incorporate action and dialogue among the youth researchers. They also had freedom to determine what forms of data they wanted to incorporate (e.g., photos from fieldtrips, interview clips, and observation sheets) and how they would use that data to convince the viewer of the importance of their makerspace. They were allowed to use written text, music, and transition effects to make their movies compelling and appealing. The young people were divided into four groups, each of which created a short movie. Table 3.1 outlines the four movies.

The construction of these movies took a significant amount of time. The youth sketched their movies, wrote scripts, and looked across their data to find evidence that they felt was compelling to their points. For example, Annabeth, Ivy, and Rayna created a movie they entitled *Makerspace, Makerspace, We Want a Makerspace*. The three girls who made this movie began by playing with power tools and filming themselves in Photo Booth playing with the tools and riffing on their ideas about a makerspace. They produced several nearly identical scenes in terms of talk, although each one showed the girls interacting with different power tools (see Figure 3.2). In all of these scenes, which made their way into their 2-minute movie, they voiced the importance of having opportunities to learn, to use a wide range of tools, and to make things that will help the world become a better place. They also emphasized the importance of access to these things for kids. As one scene described:

Rayna: Kids should have access to makerspaces at their clubs
Annabeth: It's fun!
Ivy: They can make things that save the world!
Rayna: And it keeps kids learning!
Ivy: Yeah!!!!
Rayna: Oh yeah!

As the girls became more animated in their moviemaking, they began chanting "Makerspace, makerspace, we want a makerspace!" By the end of their production, the whole room of youth voluntarily began changing the mantra with them, jumping up and down, as the camera zoomed around the room.

Manifesto. When the four groups completed their tasks, we asked them to present their movies to the whole group. After they had all

Table 3.1. Youth's YPAR Makerspace Movies

Movie	Authors	Main Themes	Critical Evidence
We Need a Makerspace . . . the Movie	Patricia and Ashlee	• Teach others about the need for a dedicated makerspace to allow them to "learn, create, and build" • The importance of colorful, safe, and welcoming space • Tools and materials for their projects	• Images of girls interviewing makerspace staff • Summary of observational findings • Challenges of a nondedicated making space
Makerspace, Makerspace, We Want a Makerspace	Annabeth, Ivy, and Rayna	• The importance of opportunities to make to "save the world" • The need for access to and opportunities to learn with power tools • Girls as makers	• Images of girls with power tools • Short videos of things they have made or would like to make • Images and explanations of makerspace tools and projects • Videos of YPAR youth stating "We want a makerspace"
What Is a Makerspace?	Lilly, Macy, and Jennifer	• Design of a safe and welcoming place to create • Youth-authored definitions of a makerspace	• Summary of interview findings • A youth-written definition
Imagine the Things We Could Make	Dan, Samuel and Christopher	• Show others youth's possibilities: If we made these things without a makerspace, imagine what we could make with one!	• Images of projects that the youth have made over several years

Figure 3.2. Girls with Power Tools

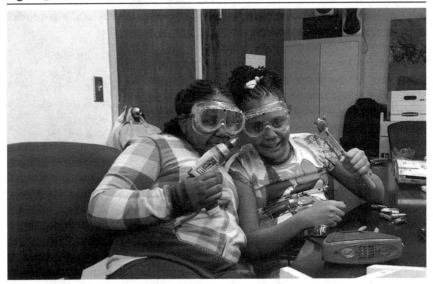

watched the four movies together, one of the mentors, Day, encouraged the young people to call out their definition of a makerspace, based on their research and their experience of making the movies:

> *Day:* We do need to come up with a definition of what a makerspace is.
> *Lilly:* Can I do more than one?
> *Day:* There could be more than one definition. Maybe we can make a combined definition, [using] all the data we've collected.
> *Macy:* A place where people can invent.
> *Day:* A place where people can invent! That's Macy. Should we write this all down?
> *[All youth and mentors]:* Yeah!

The conversation led to a spontaneous, collective production of a Makerspace Manifesto. Lilly, one of the young people, asked Day whether they could offer more than one definition of a makerspace, because she believed there were a number of critical ideas that should be included in the definition. Many of the youth began to simultaneously chime in their agreement on this point, and they decided to create a "combined definition" of a makerspace, which we named a "manifesto." One of the mentors, Day, began to record these ideas on her computer, which was projecting onto the classroom screen. The outcome was "Our Makerspace Manifesto."

OUR MAKERSPACE MANIFESTO

[To us, a makerspace is] A place where you can invent, have fun, and make stuff to save the world. You can gather to create and learn, using green energy. It should be open to all kids at the Club, so we can learn and have fun, with room for little kids AND for big kids.

It should be kid-friendly, colorful, and have a lot of space and things that you can make stuff with, like a lot of tools, lockers, computers/tablets, 3-D printers, safety goggles/gloves, a first aid kit, safety precautions, and instructions/rules/schedules on whiteboard and chalkboard walls too. And whiteboard tables, chalkboard doors, storage carts, snacks, sliding "teacher chairs" with wheels and armrests, and shelves under the tables, and lots of power outlets on tables and hanging from the ceiling with extension cords, so we don't have to go all around the room, and we can just stay where we're working and get more work done.

The University already has one. Our Club doesn't have one and kids should have more opportunities like that. Most kids don't. Instead of people asking, "What's a makerspace?" they will know because it's open to ALL kids. And the kids will tell their parents and their parents will tell their friends, and their friends will tell the whole entire world from generation to generation. And it's all because of us.

The writing of the manifesto was not a planned activity, but rather one that emerged out of what seemed to be the youth's frustration about feeling like their ideas, desires, and hopes for making and makerspaces stood in contrast to how they experienced the broader maker movement, and how they were positioned as young people in that movement.

Cutting across the manifesto and the movies were three key messages that the young people hoped to share with community members about making and makerspaces.

First, they defined *what a makerspace is for*. They viewed a makerspace as more than a workspace in which they could design and build gadgets or crafts. As can be seen in the first paragraph of the manifesto ("A place where you can invent, have fun, and make stuff to save the world," "You can gather to create and learn using green energy"), the young people viewed a makerspace as a place in which they could *make/invent something for the public good, while also having "fun."* From earlier conversations with the youth, having "fun" in STEM meant "doing science that matters" and "doing things that make a difference." During their interviews with staff at local makerspaces, they noticed that most participants in or visitors to makerspaces engaged in making for "their school projects," "hobbies," or "profit." However, our young people wanted to highlight the importance of making for their communities.

Second, they described *whom a makerspace is for.* As noted in the first and third paragraphs of the manifesto, the young people declared that a new makerspace should be built in and *open to all* in the community ("It should be open to all kids . . . " "the University already has one. Our Club doesn't have one, and kids should have more opportunities like that."). During their visits to local makerspaces, they heard from the staff or managers that those makerspaces were designed for "adults," including college students and science museum staff, not for young people or kids. They saw it as a problem that "most kids don't" have opportunities to access makerspaces in their community. By constructing a new makerspace in the community club, in which many of the young people in their city spend a lot of time after school, they hoped to see more young people or children get to know about makerspaces and to experience making in those spaces.

Last, the young people described *what a makerspace they hoped to build in their club looked like,* details of which are included in the second paragraph of the manifesto. For example, they emphasized "colorful" design to create a more welcoming, youth-friendly environment. They pointed out that "grown-up makerspaces" were not colorful, which gave the impression that working in the space was "serious," not "fun." They also underscored "safety." In local makerspaces, they had seen a lot of "things we couldn't touch," such as hardware tools or machines with sharp edges or parts, which might restrict their participation and activity. Thus, they wanted to see "safety goggles/gloves," "a first aid kit," and "safety precautions" in a youth-centered makerspace.

The youth expected to have furniture or equipment in the makerspace that would enable them to collaborate with one another easily and to work efficiently—points quite similar to the ones made in the literature cited earlier. During their virtual tour of makerspaces in other cities via the Internet and fieldtrips to local makerspaces, the young people had seen some makerspaces with large whiteboards on the wall, so that anyone in the space could write down or visualize their ideas and share them with others. To facilitate brainstorming ideas or discussing design problems with their peers and mentors, the young people hoped to have facilities such as "whiteboard and chalkboard walls," "whiteboard tables," and "chalkboard doors." They also wanted to have power outlets hanging from the ceiling with extension cords, like those they had seen in their investigations, and "sliding 'teacher chairs' with wheels and armrests," so that they could choose to work in one place or move around to work with others.

Furthermore, cutting across these key messages were four ways the youth wished to communicate these messages to others: Teach, Show, Design, and Make. Both these messages and themes, which are described below, became organizing themes for the remainder of their YPAR project.

Teach others what a makerspace is and why the youth wished to have a dedicated makerspace at their club. Patricia and Ashlee's movie shared above had a strong "teach" theme, as they used their movie to tell others about what a makerspace is. Their movie provides a definition of a makerspace, and shows close-up images of people doing things in makerspace. It highlights tools, signage, activities, and artifacts. It foregrounds what "could be" different about a youth-friendly makerspace.

Show the community what youth can do in the makerspace. The movie that Samuel, Christopher, and Dan made presented images of "inventions" they had made at the club "without a makerspace" and left the viewer with the question "Imagine what we could invent if we had a makerspace!?"

Design a youth-friendly makerspace using a digital design tool to show others what the youth wished their potential makerspace to look like. Jennifer, Lilly, and Macy's movie bridged both Teaching and Making, as they described what makerspaces are and why they are important for kids. As they stated, "In makerspaces kids and adults learn how to use their creativity to make awesome inventions. . . . It is important for kids to have a safe and welcoming place to learn." As they talked more about their movie in their video diaries and conversation groups, they expressed more strongly that how kids are supported in being creative and in feeling welcomed was tied to how the space "allowed a kid to make."

Make—Why making is important to the youth and how they wished to make. Annabeth, Rayna, and Ivy's movie had a strong design theme, as they used their movie to describe what the makerspace might look like, and the kinds of things it might include. Rayna's reflection on the movie was sharply focused on the importance of her holding the power screwdriver throughout the movie (she can be seen holding and turning on the power screwdriver in each of the scenes). She said that was important because she had not used a power tool before, and it is important for kids to have access to the things they need to make the inventions they need to "save the world."

Designing a Workshop: Teach, Show, Design, and Make!

The youth used these themes to design a workshop for the club leadership.

Teach Group. This group, comprised of Patricia and Ashlee, focused on explaining what a makerspace is and why the young people needed a makerspace in their club. The youth in the Teach Group thought carefully about what they wanted to include in their segment of the workshop. As we can see from their planning documents, they felt it was important to help their audience "feel" the way they feel when they make things. As they scripted their presentation, they wrote:

> When we make stuff, we feel awesome because it makes you feel like you can do stuff and you have the power. Everybody needs to feel that feeling. Everybody needs to know how that feels. . . . If you start young, you'll get better while you're in school and you'll learn faster and get your degree and get into a better school that teaches you better engineering information. And you need to follow your dreams. If you want to be in engineering, follow your dreams.

They also guessed that few board members would know the definition of a makerspace, just like many people in the community. Their plan was to teach the club leadership and thereby encourage them to support building a new makerspace in their club. The young people first edited the movies they had created earlier, and combined them to ensure they would send out clear messages. Their movie particularly emphasized that they would not want an "adult-friendly" makerspace but a "kid-friendly" makerspace that was more "colorful," and "a safe place and welcoming place." It also highlighted that all kids should have access to the makerspace at the club, because it allowed them to have "fun," to make something "to save the world," and to keep them "learning." In addition to the movie, this group created a PowerPoint presentation, in which they introduced the process and the results of their YPAR project, in order to emphasize that their ideas came from their own research on makerspaces.

The young people also decided to devise a number of interactive activities ("Makerspace Challenge Game"), to allow board members to experience how the children may "feel" when they engage in making in the makerspaces, and how they learn STEM-related ideas or practices in the makerspace. For instance, the young people gave the board members the opportunity to use littleBits, a system of electronic modules that snap together with magnets, to understand how electric circuits work. Board members were asked to build electric circuits with the littleBits kits, to turn on lights or activate buzzers.

Show Group. This group, comprised of Christopher, Dan, Quentin, and Samuel, focused on showing the board members what youngsters can make in makerspaces, in the hope of helping the board members to understand the importance of building a new makerspace in the club. The group first decided to introduce a couple of inventions that some of them had developed in the previous year in their maker program, such as a wind-powered anti-bully jacket, a solar-powered birdhouse, and a human-powered light-up umbrella. They created a PowerPoint presentation that included photos of their inventions and descriptions of what each invention was for, how it worked, and what green energy it used as its power source. For example, they presented the wind-powered anti-bully jacket, named the "Phantom Jacket," designed for "keep[ing] people safe," and described how it works ("If you hit the alarm, it lets other people know we are in trouble"), emphasizing that the jacket is powered by wind.

The message to board members here was that, in a new makerspace, the young people would want to *make within and for their community*. By actively responding to local/global social or community issues (e.g., bullying, climate change) by their making/engineering designs in the new makerspace, they hoped to contribute to developing their community. The makerspace for them would be a place that supported them in making a difference within and for their community. The last slide in their PowerPoint made the point explicitly ("These are ways to help our community! Help us to get a better makerspace for our future!!!").

Design Group. This group, comprised of Macy, Rayna, Jennifer, Lilly, Caitlyn, and Fall, created designs to show the board members what they want their makerspace to be like. The designs were based on the data they had collected, and were intended to allow the board members to actually "see" the makerspace. The group used a digital design tool called Google SketchUp. Rayna described what she drew in her design as follows:

> Here is a thinking couch plus a dancing couch plus a trampoline. You can jump on the trampoline to help you think. There are tables with outlets on them. There is a sink to wash your hands. And there is a whiteboard and there is a printer, a 3-D printer. And laptops right here and doughnuts and Starbucks coffee. And there is a cabinet right here.

Interestingly, Rayna's comment reminds us why it is important to incorporate young people's own perspective into designing makerspaces. Rayna was well aware that young people could not work in makerspaces "all the time." She believed that they sometimes need time to "think," which sitting on "a thinking couch" or "dancing" or "jumping on a trampoline" could help them to do. Rayna also pointed out that the new makerspace had to have a snack bar, as Rayna and many of her friends had found that they could not actively engage in making in the makerspace at the club because they were hungry after school.

Make Group. This group, comprised of Annabeth, Ivy, and Rayna (who moved back and forth between the Design and Make groups), focused on developing a 3-D model of parts of the new makerspace (e.g., equipment or furniture). During their research, they had seen a 3-D model of a makerspace created by college students. Although the Design Group planned to visualize their new makerspace, some of the young people said it would be a good idea to make 3-D models of equipment or furniture that would be placed in the new makerspace, to bring the impression of the space to life more clearly.

Using playdough, a cardboard box, and LEGO toys, this group created mini 3-D models of the makerspace and the furniture and equipment that they wanted placed in it. For example, they made a table with a whiteboard on top, which would enable people to visualize and share their ideas. They also made shelves on which they could store tools, materials, or works in progress. On the wall of the model of the makerspace hung "helpful signs." All the furniture and equipment was colorful. The young people even made an outside space with "a pool," "a thinking trampoline," and "a bounce house," so that they could work but also "have fun" at the same time.

The three girls in the group also wrote a script that described their 3-D model. Though I will not include the full script here, it is important to note the enduring themes that move from the earlier videos, to the manifesto, to their 3-D space: (a) safe, welcoming and colorful spaces to learn; (b) access to tools to think and make; and (c) being able to do things that make a difference. As one part of the script describes:

> Let's ask one of the students what they are doing!
> Tell me about what you're doing in here?
> We're building new things in our makerspace. We're using drills and computers to design things, 3-D printer to print out some of the materials that we need.
> Do you see the signs on the walls?
> These are to keep us safe and learn how to use certain tools and equipment, and they keep the room colorful and happy!
> We have made lots of things. A light-up umbrella, an alarm jacket, a bully app, a light-up football, and a phantom jacket!

After 2 and a half weeks of research and planning, the 16 youth presented their findings to the executive board of directors of their after-school club (see Figure 3.3). During the presentation, Ashlee and Patricia, two of the youth members of the program, introduced why they needed a new makerspace in the after-school club, and they appealed for support from the board members. They underlined the importance of the early making experiences that empowered them to craft their future in engineering. They also highlighted the key role of the makerspace in providing people in their community with access to the tools or materials necessary to build something they wanted or needed. Ashlee and Patricia emphasized the inclusive culture of makerspace by stating that all community members and not just makers could engage in the space.

Figure 3.3. YPAR Workshop on Makerspaces

Demonstrating their movies, PowerPoint slides, and their new designs for makerspaces that were created with a 3-D design software program and demonstrated with playdough, the youth reported what they investigated about local makerspaces, how they conducted the investigations, and what they discovered during the process. In addition, they conducted an interactive activity in which the board members could experience a simple making process, such as building electric circuits to operate a motor or to turn on buzzers. Although the youth had only half an hour to present their works to the executive board members, they created a space where their voices and experiences on makerspaces were heard and shared. Drawing upon their research, the youth challenged the traditional notion of makerspaces being only for adult hobbyists or engineering college students, and they sought to build a new youth-centered and community-based makerspace in their after-school club. Surprisingly, a few weeks later, the youth heard that the board members decided to expand the after-school club's building area for a new makerspace, and the board members planned to allocate the necessary budget funds for buying the machines, tools, and materials needed for the space. See Table 3.2 for a summary of these critical events.

DISCUSSION

The story of the youth in this study shows how young people framed the importance of youth-centered and community-based makerspaces

Table 3.2. Critical Events

Critical Events	Main Activities	Key Insights/ Turning Points
Investigation into makerspaces (16 hours)	• Youth constructed interview and observational protocols, and visited local makerspaces in person and makerspaces across the country virtually.	• A strong critique of the maker movement emerged, with youth highlighting critical themes around youth-friendly versus adult-friendly • Power dynamics and opportunities to make
Authoring movies about making and makerspaces (8 hours)	• Youth self-formed teams to analyze and present findings of their investigations in 3-minute videos that contained: • Explanation of what makerspaces are, and • At least four different pieces of evidence from their investigations.	• Four themes emerged that inspired the youth and mentors to codesign a workshop • Teach others what a youth-friendly makerspace is • Show others what you may accomplish with the right opportunities • Design features of a youth-friendly and equity-oriented making space • Make—how youth imagine the possibilities of making in ways that matter to them
Our Manifesto (2 hours)	• Discussion of movie themes led youth and mentors to spontaneously author a manifesto, leveraging key themes and insights.	• What a makerspace is • Who a makerspace is for • What a youth-friendly and equity-oriented makerspace looks like
Workshop (16 hours)	• Teach, Design, Make, and Show Presentations	• Synthesis of ideas of youth-friendly making spaces • Youth as key stakeholders in making space design • Youth as teachers of adults.

and how this framing ties in to who they are and who they want to be in these places. As young people, they have identified the embodied connections with the sociality and materiality of place of the makerspaces they visited (Jones & Evans, 2012) and what they meant for who they felt they could be in those spaces. At the same time, their YPAR also calls attention to the agency the youth have, individually and collectively, to construct ideas toward their hoped-for place of making, in youth-oriented and empowering ways. The findings of the study suggest two major themes on designing inclusive makerspaces for young people from nondominant communities.

First, youth critically identified how the designs of the making spaces they visited positioned them without a rightful presence. Youth were awed by the sophisticated tools in these spaces (e.g., laser cutter, different kinds of 3-D printers), but they also had strong opinions on how their own youth makerspace at their community club should *"feel* different." They worried about the fact that they could not "touch" or "experiment" with things and that these spaces were "too serious." Everything displayed looked perfect, too expensive, or too hard to use without help. They felt that adults talked down to them or "babied" them. They felt anxious in some of these spaces. They noticed that most of the people were White people, mostly men and mostly adults, and that the books and materials laying around reinforced that observation.

Indeed, their YPAR project identified a number of design features of makerspaces that marginalized the participation of young people. They noted equipment they could not touch and tools that were stored too high or were locked up. They noted a lack of spaces to think and be playful, especially when they felt frustrated. These realizations caused deep frustration among the youth, leading them to push back on the focus of the data collection so that they could delve deeper into these concerns.

Second, the young people contested the boundaries of making and makerspaces, repositioning what it meant to make and be a maker. As they critiqued, they also sought to define what a makerspace meant to them and what it meant to belong or have a rightful presence there. You heard some of this language in the video they produced, but this language showed up in the manifestos they wrote, in their workshops, and interviews: (a) What the youth were supported to do, (b) who the youth were supported to make with, and (c) how the youth were allowed to be.

The youth wished to engage in making that mattered to them, their communities, and the world. They describe making in their movies and manifesto as about "saving the world," and they linked their ability to do so with whether their makerspace had the right tools and resources. When they wrote their "Makerspace Manifesto," they put attention on what they could do. They explicitly stated in their manifesto that they wanted to "make stuff to save the world" and that they needed to "have a lot of space and things that you can make stuff with" and proceeded to name the different types of tools and resources.

At the same time, they also wanted their space to be welcoming of all people—younger and older kids, and kids with different knowledge or skill levels. They did not want anyone to be "turned away" from an activity because "they can't do it." In their manifesto they wrote, "Our Club doesn't have one [a makerspace] and kids should have more opportunities like that. Most kids don't. Instead of people asking "What's a makerspace?," they will know because it's open to ALL kids. And the kids will tell their parents and their parents will tell their friends, and their friends will tell the whole entire world from generation to generation." The youth positioned their families and community members as insiders to the makerspace that they envisioned. This was important to youth for many reasons, one of which was about giving access to a wide range of making resources to their community.

At the same time, they also wanted that access for themselves—to grant them greater access to STEM, a field that for too long has marginalized young people of color. Gaining access to STEM is not just about their futures, but their dreams for themselves and their communities: "We want to take our makerspace to the next level . . . so everybody can see how it feels to be a builder, an engineer, to make something."

Although these are all concerns about a youth-friendly space, they speak loudly to how that space must work for youth of color and youth growing up in poverty. To an extent, the youth's work deviates from the prototypical maker who is the "independent," "individualistic" "do-it-yourself" learner. Instead of being primarily motivated by their individual interests, the youth in their YPAR work defined their engagement through collectively formed interests, and often interests that carried deep meanings on issues of race, power, oppression, and danger. In their workshop they "showed" projects that defined their work—a phantom jacket meant to keep them safe as they walk, an anti-bully app that leverages crowdsourcing to share information about bully locations, and a light-up football for playing in the dark when the streetlights do not work. The youth were concerned about problems that are defined through interactions with others and leverage others' experiences and struggles—which they see themselves as a part of—toward making. These maker "projects" are distinctly different from the regular maker projects undertaken in prototypical makerspaces (e.g., projects discussed in *Make:* magazine). This collective form of engagement also speaks to the knowledge communities in which youth participate, and which cross into the makerspace: peer, family, online, STEM, and local communities.

Lastly, the findings of the YPAR project also indicate the youth's design preferences for the makerspace and how that ties in to how they are allowed to be. For example, they wanted a "colorful" design to create a *welcoming* and *fun* environment. They preferred furniture or equipment that promotes *collaboration* with others in the makerspace, such as whiteboard tables and sliding teacher chairs. The youth also emphasized the importance of having a space where they can have a "think time" by sitting on "a thinking couch," or a space where they can "dance" or "jump on a trampoline." See Table 3.3 for a summary of the youth's design preferences.

LOOKING AHEAD:
CHALLENGING THE BOUNDARIES OF MAKING AND MAKERSPACES

> When we make stuff, we feel awesome because it makes you feel like you can do stuff and you have the power. Everybody needs to feel that feeling. Everybody needs to know how that feels. . . . A lot of people want to build stuff but don't have stuff to build it with. A community makerspace offers stuff to people who need stuff to build with. They can build anything. In a community, you feel welcome. If you don't feel welcome, then you won't want to go help people build stuff. —Ashlee and Patricia

The story of the youth also shows that they challenged the traditional boundaries of making and makerspaces. The young people in the study defined makerspaces as having multilayered meanings; these spaces were tied to who the youth are, who they want to be, and what they want to do in these spaces. For example, the young people viewed makerspaces as places where they can make something "to save the world" and "for their community" as responsible members of the local/global community. Moreover, the youth did not define makerspaces as simply workspaces where they should engage solely in engineering/making; instead, they also viewed makerspaces as places to "have fun," "learn," and "think." They thus hoped for makerspaces that can act as places to support them in their participation in a variety of activities.

The youth also saw the multifaceted roles or values of making. For instance, the young people believed that making experiences in their everyday lives can empower them and allow them to feel "awesome." They wanted everybody in their community to feel the same way. They also asserted that accumulated making experiences can create a new pathway toward their future (e.g., becoming engineers). Thus, they needed a space in their community in which they can continue to participate in making.

This notion of making and makerspaces of the youth shaped what kind of makerspace they want to have in the club (simply represented as

Table 3.3. Youth's Design Preferences

Criteria	Youth's Design Criteria
Welcoming	• Colorful chairs, walls, carpets, and lockers • Lockers to keep projects safe while not being worked on • Tools not locked up • Tools and materials at heights kids can reach • Signs around the room to provide information on how to use tools
Collaborative	• Big tables • Chairs with wheels • Tables with whiteboard tops • Chalkboard walls and whiteboard walls
Fun/Playful	• Colorful • Dance floor • Music • Disco ball • Snacks • Couch, hammock, or beanbag chairs • Games
Recognizing difficult nature of work	• Thinking station that one could use at any time • A place to hang up "mess-ups" (to show other kids it is okay to mess up) • A playful space to blow off frustrations/steam
Iteration	• Hanging up rough drafts/mess-ups • Flexible flow—go to thinking station whenever you want
Making a difference	• Invites community • Projects that "save the world" • Hang up/display previous projects like "phantom jacket"

"a youth-centered and community-based makerspace"). The young people believed that "adult-friendly" makerspaces do not allow them to be who they want to be or do what they want to do, so they took initiatives to design and create a new makerspace in their community.

This finding implies that if we want to design or develop inclusive makerspaces for the youth, we need to first understand their perceptions of making and makerspaces. As illustrated in this chapter, such views may be deeply connected to who these young people are, who they want to be, and what they want to do in the makerspace, which may be different from the desires of adults or outsiders.

The criteria named by the youth in their vision for a makerspace push back against a movement that has positioned them as outsiders. Few studies on makerspaces have positioned the youth as the key stakeholders or subjects in the discourse of designing inclusive makerspaces. Most studies consider young people as simply visitors in makerspaces or as objects of study. Although researchers and practitioners have attempted to collaborate in designing inclusive makerspaces, little research that empowers the youth in participating in the development of inclusive makerspaces has been conducted.

In this chapter, the youth's stories highlight the importance of involving young people as key stakeholders in discussions of the equity issues of makerspaces and suggests how researchers and educators can support youth in participating in such discussions. The 16 youth who joined the YPAR project proved that they possessed "revealing wisdom" (Fine, 2008, p. 215) in their deconstruction of the power dynamics embedded in "adult-friendly" makerspaces, which have historically marginalized the participation of youth from nondominant communities. Furthermore, these young people reconstructed the notion of makerspace (as "youth-centered and community-based") throughout the YPAR.

When designing makerspaces, youth should be involved (work w/ kids, not for them)

CHAPTER 4

Youth as Community Ethnographers
Making Space for Community Knowledge and Wisdom

> We want to make stuff that we can't even imagine at [our community making space]. We want to learn more ways to help our community.
>
> —Kayla and Kairee, 7th-graders

In this chapter we investigate community ethnography as pedagogy as an approach to equity-oriented making. As we noted in the previous chapter, research studies within the making movement have shed important insights into the design of making spaces and its relationship to supporting making practices. We are particularly interested in the design principle of community ethnography as pedagogy. Generally, community ethnography as pedagogy is a stance that suggests that community perspectives, knowledge, and wisdom matter. It is also a stance that considers the importance of expanding opportunities for where, when, and how youth make, while incorporating youth's diverse interests and ways of being in the world.

However, we are deeply aware that community ethnography as pedagogy is a collaboratively constructed ideal—one that involves multiple perspectives and locations in the world, from the youth, to parents and community elders, to STEM educators and experts. Whose voices matter in making? How might community input, insight, and wisdom be recruited to inform youth's making projects, so that youth can "make for the common good," as Kayla and Kairee have described their making endeavors? Making for the common good necessitates co-defining with the community the whats, whys, hows, and whens of making that can meet a community need.

Thus, in this chapter, we take up the following two questions: (1) What is community ethnography as pedagogy and what roles may it play in supporting youth in the coconstruction of new making practices and positions? (2) How does community ethnography support making space educators and researchers in learning more about youth concerns and desires for making and the cultural practices they bring to making?

YOUTH AS COMMUNITY ETHNOGRAPHERS

The recruitment of community is germane from the equity-oriented stance we outlined in Chapters 1 and 2. Beyond the geographical locale in which the making space is physically situated, communities' shared lives link past histories with the everyday, including how entrenched inequities have been visited upon communities and manifested through time. To authentically engage and push back on inequities in youth's lives, we argue that engaging in and with community is a *nonnegotiable*. Thus, we have been particularly interested in community-centered making, and this is the primary reason we sought to work with our partners. In particular, we are interested in supporting and learning alongside youth in their work as community ethnographers, as an integral part of their making process.

As described in Chapter 2, community-centeredness carried *three* interrelated meanings in our work that have direct bearing on ethnography that we will briefly note again here. First, the making spaces were housed in community centers and followed norms for participation reflective of those community spaces. For example, programs were inter-age (generally ages 10–15), supported flexible movement in and out of programs due to transient life circumstances while also promoting sustained engagement, and involved youth in ongoing codesign of experiences. Second, the two focal making programs sought to create spaces for youth to interact with the broader community served by the youth clubs. These communities include the schools the youth attended and the neighborhoods they lived in. Third, making space educators periodically designed activities or events that brought community members from the larger community, including local universities and businesses, into the community center to provide feedback or help on projects.

Operating from the assumption that all communities make and have rich resources relevant to making, we deem it essential to consider how communities can contribute to community-focused youth making spaces and to their continual support (Green, 2015). Gathering community input, so that the making space would be "true to the community," is key, especially when there is no clear model of a community-focused, youth-driven making space. One way to gather such community data is by engaging in community ethnography.

Ethnography as a research methodology originated in the field of anthropology and has been described as a way of studying "lived cultures" (Gray, 2002). There is an immersion in the world one is observing, as one engages as a participant observer, to understand how people inhabit that world and negotiate social interactions (Tedlock, 1991; Watson & Till, 2010). It is important to note, however, that the roots of anthropology (and ethnography) are entangled with those of imperialism, and predicated in "otherness" and "difference" (Said, 1989). Historically, the ethnographer/anthropologist, invariably a member of the metropole, descends among the colonized to study and document the ways of the "uncivilized." The collected ethnographic data are then sorted and categorized into analytical bits, labeled as "structure," "practice," and "meaning" (Simpson, 2007) of someone else's lived culture, often deemed as inferior, when defined against the superior core of the metropole (Said, 1989).

Even as we acknowledge the affordances of an ethnographic approach toward a more holistic understanding of social practices within particular cultures, we think it crucial to note the overtly political and imperialistic underpinnings of anthropology and ethnography. We therefore take seriously the notion that sovereignty matters, and that it matters equally "at the level of method and representation" (Simpson, 2007, p. 70).

Positioning and equipping the youth as community ethnographers was one way in which we sought to guard against imperialistic overtures or undertones in our collaborative work, especially given our equity-oriented goals. This undertaking is necessarily complex, because as academics trained in qualitative research we are the ones with the expertise in ethnographic research methodology. The youth, however, are the insiders of their communities, with insider wisdom and insider radars that pick up on signals that are not apparent to an outsider ethnographer, in spite of the fact that we have worked alongside the youth in their communities for years (Taylor & Hall, 2013).

As insiders, Ozer (2016) argues, engaging in critical ethnographic research processes, youth can critique the injustices meted out by more powerful others in their communities, including their residential neighborhoods, schools, and their future working lives. Morell (2006) further notes how such critiques cut across areas such as gentrification, stereotypes and minimal living wage negotiations. Through community ethnography youth can be empowered to begin to "de-normalize" the injustices they experience through a more informed framing of the forces that precipitate such injustices, and to craft an agentic response that can bring about positive change (Rubel et al., 2017). In these studies, youth chiefly operate from the stance of a youth researchers exploring existing societal inequities. However, how youth move from understanding inequality through their participatory action research to taking informed action to make change is often fraught with uncertainty, and muddled up in relations of power.

Although it could be argued that the youth, through engaging in ethnography of their own communities, are involved in a form of auto-ethnography (Hayano, 1979), we consider community ethnography a more accurate descriptor given the different types of communities (e.g., club, school, home, neighborhood, online environment) youth engage with as a part of their making process. Auto-ethnography also alludes to an insider exploring an already established culture, which is not the case at either site, since the youth and their community collaborators were collectively working out what a community-based, youth-focused making space entailed.

COMMUNITY ETHNOGRAPHY AS PEDAGOGY IN MAKING

Pedagogies shape how people are welcomed, positioned, and recognized in making spaces, which in turn shape the opportunities youth have to learn and become in these making spaces. We are interested in relationalities in pedagogy—the I, thou, it (Hawkins, 1974), and the undergirding philosophical view related to why we do what we do, and how it aligns with our goals for being together in a space. We sought to enact community ethnography as pedagogy to expand opportunities for youth to make in ways that incorporate youth's diverse interests and ways of being in the world, the critiques those experiences bring to bear, and the agency to make a difference.

Supporting youth in becoming community ethnographers of their own communities entailed the youth learning research methods to be participant observers of the worlds that they inhabit. Through community ethnography, youth investigate their communities, STEM, and making concurrently to build a more just world. Because they are grounded in efforts to unpack community experience in visual, embodied, and connected ways (Heath, 2012), students will have opportunities to see their concerns as issues larger than personal interests, which has been shown to promote more robust participation (Zeldin, 2004).

Positioning and supporting youth as community ethnographers is an explicit pedagogical goal of community ethnography as pedagogy. We sought to help position youth as insider experts who are co-owners of collective community wisdom for not only framing making, but also for potentially disrupting the systems of inequalities they experience. Community ethnography as pedagogy can also broaden who the stakeholders are in their making process. This approach is consistent with the National Research Council's (2010) recommendation that engineering education utilize more community-based forms of research. Historically, students have been the ones researched by others in community ethnographies (Duffy & Bailey, 2010).

Ethnographic tools provide useful and unique insight into local knowledge in contextually meaningful ways. Thus, a central aspect of community ethnography as pedagogy is creating opportunities for youth makers and their mentors, throughout the making process, to leverage tools that support them in (a) careful observation of people and phenomena and the relationships among them, (b) interviewing and

[handwritten margin note: goal to frame making + disrupt systems of inequities]

conversational techniques that engage others in dialogue, and (c) capturing images of people and phenomena of interest. For example, throughout the making process, youth conduct interviews and surveys with club peers and staff members, university personnel (including teacher educators, graduate students, making space mentors), and family/community members in their residential neighborhoods. They also hold community forums and feedback sessions, welcoming community members into their making space to provide input on their work. These tools are applied toward generating a range of multiple perspectives, including local community knowledge (e.g., peers, parents, community members) and expert science/engineering knowledge (e.g., science teachers, energy experts, engineers, government officials). We conjecture that who constitutes the "we," how we can be together in what particular scenarios and across which spaces, doing what kinds of activities, could be made more tangible and experiential through community ethnography.

We would be remiss if we did not also work to intentionally and consistently weave in opportunities for young people to work toward deepening STEM knowledge and practices in support of robust STEM-rich making. The maker movement has been critiqued, and rightly so, for potentially increasing the inequalities in STEM because it may further position those with the technical know-how to build upon that, while leaving others to make in less technically robust ways. This is a particular challenge as we seek to employ approaches to deepening STEM in ways that disrupt rather than advance knowledge and power hierarchies. The question we faced was how could we support youth in learning the STEM they may need, as they engage in more technically robust making (e.g., power requirements, energy transformations, circuits, etc.), in ways that are informed by their community knowledge, practice, and wisdom.

Thus, integrated across community ethnography as pedagogy is what we refer to as codesigned "just-in-time" STEM experiences (JiTs), on an as-needed basis, when STEM knowledge gaps are surfaced through community ethnography. The goal of JiTs is to allow youth to work toward more robust STEM-rich making projects that more fully respond to the needs they identify and sharpen as they engage in making and ethnographic work. JiTs are short, emergent experiences meant to teach in-the-moment, critical content and practices that youth may need as they engage in more technically robust making (e.g., power requirements, energy transformations, circuits, etc.). However, unlike front-loading STEM content knowledge before making happens by the STEM expert teaching others, as is typical in formal STEM classes, these are co-initiated and codesigned experiences that arise because they have been identified by youth, their mentors, or members of the community with whom they interact during the making process as being important in their making projects. Sometimes JiTs are designed and led by community members.

For example, when one group of youth sought to hack a baby gate in order to motorize it to help elderly caregivers, one of the youth's fathers was recruited to help with his knowledge of minimal-damage, furniture take-apart techniques. Sometimes they are led by mentors and youth as they seek to collaboratively figure out how to address a technical challenge, such as when a mentor and two girls sought to figure out how to construct a multicircuit so that their light-up scooter could be seen from the end of the block, a problem one of the moms stated was important to their project. However, they are always initiated by a need to know as youth dig more deeply into the problems and possible responses to the problems they seek to address.

COMMUNITY ETHNOGRAPHY TOWARD NEW PRACTICES AND SPACES OF MAKING

We integrate community ethnography across the making process. However, we frame the role of ethnography differently at different stages of making. Early on in the making process, we frame ethnography as critical engagement around the problems that matter ("mapping the problem space through community dialogues"). This involves youth naming and critiquing injustices in their communities that have consequences in their future. Critical engagement also entails youth moving from unpacking and understanding inequalities that concern them, to taking informed action. We are particularly concerned with how youth may interact with and gain insights from a wide range of community members as they seek to figure out what problems they want to address through their making.

Later, as youth turn ideas into projects, we frame community ethnography toward designs that bridge knowledges and experiences ("merging epistemologies and shared ownership in design"). Here we consider the following critical questions: (1) Who is their making project for? (2) Whose knowledge counts in their making project? (3) Who takes part in defining the problem, in data collection, in interpretation and data analysis? (4) Who owns the making project, and to what ends? We are concerned with supporting youth in using community ethnography in ways that support and contribute to the STEM dimensions of their designs. STEM and community knowledge are usually viewed as coming from different epistemological locations, and so finding ways to support youth in bridging these is especially important in community-centered making.

To illustrate how community ethnography with youth unfolds, below we describe the approaches we use, bringing in examples from different projects. These approaches are summarized in Table 4.1.

[handwritten margin notes:] 1st step is critical engagement where students define problems that matter

2nd step is creating designs that bridge knowledge + experience

Mapping the Problem Space Through Community Dialogues

From a STEM-rich making perspective, youth makers need support in figuring out how to move from a topic (e.g., transportation concerns, toy safety, etc.) to a problem space where they can develop realistic and testable projects and tools based upon current knowledge, empirical investigation of technical and social dimensions, and operational constraints and specifications (e.g., What devices can I build to get me to my friend's house when my parents cannot take me?). However, from a community-centered and equity-oriented perspective, youth also need opportunities to bridge how they understand both the technical and sociocultural dimensions of the problems they hope to solve through making. This joint process involves (1) identifying community problems that STEM-rich making can solve, and what one needs to know about the technology to solve the problem (e.g., Can I adapt my scooter to have solar-powered lights? Can it work in the dark?) and (2) identifying a range of relevant perspectives in both the engineering and local communities (e.g., parents, teachers, safety officers, scooter design experts, solar energy experts, etc.) and evaluating their impact on the design process. This latter component requires the translation of technical language into questions, ideas, and concerns that relevant stakeholders will understand. Likewise, it involves mapping sociocultural concerns and insights back onto technical considerations.

To support youth makers in *defining problems* in ways that incorporate technical and sociocultural dimensions and their interactions, we have designed a set of maker learning experiences through community ethnography: Mapping the problem space through community dialogues, (a) framing the problems that matter and (b) refining the problem space. Through these experiences youth learn to integrate community dialogues with surveys and observations toward better understanding the concerns and wisdom of their communities and how that maps onto their own concerns.

Framing Problems That Matter

Generating insights: Youth dialogues. Each year, a theme for the maker programs is set based on ideas that youth bring forward. In this initial process, we work with youth to surface their collective experience in both its realities (which include the inequities they may face and their collective community wisdom toward naming those problems). To do this we begin the year with a set of youth dialogues and with mapping activity on the topic. For example, during the unit in which we focused on transportation, we started with the prompt "Tell a story about the challenges you have encountered in transportation; What are some inventions you wish you had to help you with your challenges?" As youth tell their stories, we collectively build a conceptual map of their stories, marking physical, geographical, political, cultural, and symbolic connections across the stories. Narrative is a powerful tool in ethnography, and for us it is important to start with the youth's stories before we build out into the community.

Generally, this process takes several sessions, and as the maps become more detailed, youth take time alone or in small groups to individually map out new ideas that the conversations have raised for them. In their small groups, youth step back to reflect on the community they are serving in their making, and how they are a part of that community —their memberships, roles, activities, and experiences. They are then asked to layer the ideas from the youth dialogues and mapping activity onto insights from their community—for example: What are the specific challenges members of this community face, and how do they connect to the challenges you face? Which idea do you think is most important and why? What are three things you need to learn more about regarding this problem?

Take, for example, Caitlyn and Quentin's concern with their cellphone batteries dying during the school day. At the beginning of the school year, the two youth members were asked by their maker-mentors to brainstorm problems that they encountered throughout the year and that they wished to solve by means of STEM-rich making. As mentors, we worked closely with Caitlyn and Quentin to facilitate a larger discussion with peers to solicit their input. One of the problems that surfaced was that many of the young people were concerned with the "short life of cellphone batteries."

In reflecting on this dialogue, Caitlyn and Quentin described a variety of ways they and their peers used cellphones in their everyday lives. Caitlyn, for example, noted: "When I am out with my friends, and my phone dies, and I need to get in touch with my mom, then I have no way to charge it."

Quentin also illustrated another important role of cellphones: " . . . Phones are the new computers, social networks, GPS." Like many of his peers growing up in lower-income households, Quentin has a smartphone and relies on it to stay connected—locally with friends and globally with the world. For youth growing up in lower-income communities, smartphones are key channels for connecting to the broader world. In fact, more than half of U.S. teenagers and young adults in lower-income brackets are smartphone owners (Smith, 2015). For these young people, the cellphone is their landline, Internet connection, calculator, translator, camera, encyclopeia, and email all-in-one device. Quentin and his peers use their phones for their schoolwork, social networking, and navigation. Quentin's and Caitlyn's comments articulate the needs their community faces as well as the ethical considerations they are willing to tackle. For Caitlyn, Quentin, and their peers, keeping their smartphones working is crucial.

Caitlyn and Quentin also recognized youth's difficulties in keeping their cellphones charged, especially outside or during the school day when there is limited (or no) access to electrical outlets. As Quentin pointed out, youth "keep their cellphones on all the time." Although they try to charge their phones at home overnight, their phones usually die by early afternoon because of the short battery life. In addition, as Caitlyn noted, youth struggle to find places to charge their cellphones, and once they find such places, they have to "wait there" until the charging is finished, unable to move along with their friends. This makes Caitlyn feel "desperate."

Caitlyn and Quentin were aware that their parents, friends, and neighbors had experienced the same problem. As Caitlyn said, "My parents, my community, my friends, they are always running out of phone battery." Indeed, the youth defined their design problem based not solely on their own interests and needs but also on the concerns and needs of their community, illustrating their willingness to engage in engineering design to solve problems larger than their own.

Generating insights: Surveys. As youth share their ideas about the most important problems and what they want to learn about them, they are then tasked with constructing short surveys to help them to engage in dialogue on these issues with members of their community.

We always start with a list of starter questions, which includes questions about how the people they talk to are positioned within their community, the challenges these individuals identify as important, and insights they have on the challenges the youth have identified as important:

- Please describe who you are: parent, kid, teenager, community member, teacher/staff.
- What are some challenges you face in your everyday life?
- What are some challenges your community faces?
- Can you tell me more about this challenge? How come people haven't been able to solve it?
- How important is the issue of [fill in the challenge you identified here]?
- Who do you think we should talk to for more information about who might be affected by this problem of interest?

Youth modify these starter questions to include questions they care about, and to ensure that the language connects to who they are and how they want to talk to others. We also work with the youth to practice how they would use the survey to open up dialogue with community members. The goal here is not only to gather insights on the questions in the survey, but also to have an exchange of ideas around the survey questions.

Take, for example, Samuel, who ultimately designed a wind-powered anti-bully jacket called "a phantom jacket" in his community making space. When Samuel designed his phantom jacket, he hoped it would make people in his community "feel safe on the streets at night."

Initially, Samuel and his peers identified safety as the issue they wanted to address. He and his peers shared stories about bullying, needing to stay warm, being seen at night, staying dry in the snow and rain, children getting hurt in the home, home security, and a wide range of health issues as important topics related to safety. Samuel's main concern was bullying within his peer group. He worried about being bullied, something that he had experienced in the past. He did not identify an anti-bullying jacket as a potential project, however, until he surveyed members of his community.

Samuel and his friends developed a seven-item survey, with the following questions: "What are some of your safety concerns?" "Where are the areas that you think safety is most important?" and "What are some ideas that can help you solve those safety concerns?" Then, using an online survey design program and a tablet, over the course of a week, he and his peers surveyed 62 people in their community, including peers and staff at the club, families, teachers, and school friends.

During the surveys, Samuel would often use individual questions as launching points to have more substantive conversations. When he was interviewing a peer about ideas on safety, he followed up the survey questions with specific comments and questions about his peer's particular experiences, as when he said, "Well, like, did it ever happen to you that you could not get help when you needed it when you were walking alone?" and "Do you think others will have this problem, too?" Samuel talked about the surveys as important because they gave him different ideas for how to think about the problem he was interested in. It also gave him new ideas on how and what to talk to people about: "So I went to go ask other people who haven't had the same answer and then I used their evidence against mine and their evidence was good, my evidence was good, so I kept asking more people."

Examining data across perspectives. Supporting youth in analyzing the data using multiple representations is important. First, we have youth graph the closed items to identify large patterns and trends and to filter those trends based on "perspective," such as kid, teen, or adult, girls or boys, etc. Graphical analysis of ethnographic data is an important approach to making visible their concerns as current and salient issues to be tackled in STEM-rich making. Codesigning and enacting their survey, then analyzing and representing their data in visible mathematical norms, imbued both power and legitimacy to their concerns in important ways. This process also helps the youth see how their own experiences align (or not) with these patterns.

Second, and more important, is helping the youth to dig into the open-ended data and use the data to unpack the trends in experience in community. To return to Samuel's story, he and his peers used a "bubble map" to flesh out the ideas (smaller bubbles) shared by community members as they related to the larger trends (large bubbles) previously identified. Through this process, Samuel discovered key safety issues that concerned his community, such as "walking" "transportation," "school," "driving," "stealing," and "food" (Figure 4.1). He noticed that even though people mentioned walking as a safety issue, it could refer to different things. That is, some people felt that walking in the streets was not safe because of pervasive gang activities. On the other hand, others believed that walking in the streets was dangerous because of the limited street-lights. Samuel also found that peers and younger children were more concerned about walking in the streets, while adults were more worried about driving on the roads.

As Samuel further analyzed the survey data, he was able to narrow down the problems he hoped to solve using engineering. When analyzing the answers to the questions of the survey, he noticed that approximately 75% of the participants "felt unsafe on the streets" as they commuted to school, home, and other places. They were interested in having things that would allow them to walk where they wanted, when they wanted. When Samuel was asked what he had learned from his analysis of the survey data, he said:

> Yeah, people walk and sometimes they say it's not safe to walk, so it's, like, 75% of people that walk and they say it's not safe to walk. So I just thought I'd make the jacket for them. And so it will keep them safe so they don't get hurt when they walk.

As we can see from the quote above, Samuel recognized that a large percentage of people in his community had the same concerns about feeling unsafe on the streets as he did.

An important part of this process is helping youth identify who they want to talk to and why, and using the surveys as opportunities for opening up dialogue with community members. To this end, we spend time working with youth to generate strategies for reaching the people they want to reach. If a group wanted to reach parents, then one strategy they might use would be to stand by the community club entrance during the most popular pick-up hours. If a group wanted to reach teachers, then we

Figure 4.1. Samuel's Bubble Map

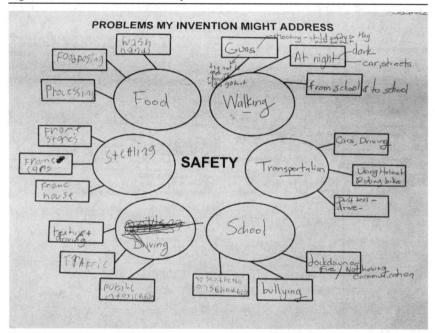

might arrange with them to walk over to the neighboring school during the 30-minute period after school when teachers are most likely to be around.

We also help youth think about how they might introduce their topic to the people they may survey as a further way of gleaning insights, for the conversations youth may have as a part of interacting around a survey are just as important as the survey itself.

To look more closely at these concerns as a part of the larger survey process, take for example the group of girls who made SafePax. SafePax, a backpack equipped with lights and an alarm, was designed by three African American girls, Lisa (11 years old), Tina (11), and Tonya (10), who self-selected into a making group out of friendship. Over several months, the SafePax group used multiple rounds of interviews and surveys with community members to formulate a project idea, and then refine it so that it served the community's needs.

During the first weeks of a new maker unit, the youth were encouraged to brainstorm with one another their own questions and concerns that they felt were good topics for taking up in a new maker project. The focus was on "safety"—a focus area decided upon by the youth themselves earlier in the year. As part of the brainstorming process, the youth were also asked to generate questions about their ideas that they could ask others—questions that they would want to be asked themselves about their project ideas. They also thought about whom they might interview (younger kids, their peers, older kids, adult staff, and parents), and why that might matter. Their final questions included: (1) What safety concerns do you have in your community? (2) What makes you feel unsafe? and (3) Where are you and what are you doing when you feel unsafe? These questions became *tools for building connections* with members of their community on shared safety concerns.

They also determined whom they might survey and why, and developed strategies for reaching their target population. As all three girls had been members of the community club for many years, with many peers not in the maker club, they decided to survey those peers. From a program standpoint, this was also convenience sampling—the girls simply needed to walk out of the making space room into the other rooms of the community club.

The girls, with the help of one of their mentors, then uploaded their top questions into an online survey platform they would use to collect data from their club community. As they practiced their interviews, they considered what they would tell others about their projects—engineering a product to address a community-identified safety issue. The girls divided the interview questions between Tonya and Trina, with Lisa preferring to be the "iPad recorder person" who would videotape the interviews. Tonya and Trina practiced articulating the questions before the girls began their interviews. As they interviewed their peers, they visited different "club rooms" each time, taking the time to talk with their peers using the survey questions as launching points into dialogue on the topics raised. Bullying at school was a common concern brought up by peers. While the girls invited friends outside of the making club to be interviewed, other peers, curious about the tablet and conversation, also joined in and the girls ended up talking to clusters of peers during their interviews. As they discussed their findings in their small group, they began to make meaning of them by relating them to personal experiences. In response to the survey responses, the girls told stories about the different issues that trigger bullying (from lack of fashion, such as "not having the right [brand] shoes," to "being called stupid" by school peers). When Lisa added that "a lot of times the teachers know about the bullying but they don't do nothing about it," Trina agreed, but added that "at my school a lot of bullying is in the girls' bathroom so there's nobody, I mean an adult, there to help you, who you gonna call for help?" This conversation led the girls to decide to work on a project that would help others if they were bullied. Then Trina excitedly recalled that she had seen a commercial on television for a "bully-proof backpack, it has a cord that you can pull and then an alarm goes off . . . my friend had one. But she pulled the cord and nothing happened." The girls decided they wanted to make their own "bully-proof backpack that has an alarm you can press to call for help, that will work and be cheaper, and can help you in the bathroom or places with no adults to call for help."

Here we can see how the youth framed the community data as powerful and important data, not as opinions or outsider views. Enacting the survey allowed the girls access to interact with peers and other members of the community with whom they did not typically come into contact, which helped them build momentum and solidarity around the pertinence of these social issues. Learning that others' concerns shared stark similarities with their own concerns about bullying further affirmed their wish to address this concern.

use interactions to help youth see multiple perspectives & see themselves relationally to others

COMMUNITY DIALOGUES AND OBSERVATIONS TOWARD REFINING THE PROBLEM SPACE

Engaging youth in thinking about gathering observational data is as much about teaching a stance as it is about gathering data. A critical part of this aspect of our approach is supporting young people to figure out what it means to be a community investigator in a space to innovate. Here, we want youth to think about what it means to look deeply at ways *people act or respond* to interactions with others and their surroundings—especially how people in their community are affected by external factors (i.e., other people, places, things, etc.). We are concerned with how the youth see themselves relationally with other people. What do they know about the people and the contexts they are observing? What is their own role in that context? How do they participate with community members to ensure that their observations reflect multiple perspectives and not just their own?

We first have youth practice making observations of the kinds of things happening in their own maker program. For example, we ask them to pick a scenario to observe and write their notes below:

- What are they doing? Who are they with? Where are they?
- Who are they talking to? What are they saying?
- Do you see them doing any hand gestures or using body language that shows emotions?
- How about eye contact?

As we talk about what they have observed, we ask them what they can infer from their observation—for example: What do they think is happening and why? Then we push them to consider the question, What other tools and approaches might help them better understand the event as it unfolds? Our goal is to help the youth see themselves as active participants in the communities they observe, engaging in dialogue and interaction with others as they seek to make sense of what may be happening. Part of this conversation is helping youth to figure out when they may hold back and when they may interact.

We then return to the problem-spaces maps they created through their surveys and dialogues and ask them to add a new layer to it by addressing the following questions: What questions has your survey analysis raised for you? What else do you want to find out? How could observation help you determine: (a) Who you want to observe, when, where, and why? (b) What questions you might ask as you are engaged in observation?

If we return to Caitlyn and Quentin's concern about the short life of cellphone batteries, we can see how observations—both formal and over time from living in their communities—of activities and needs within their community helped them refine the problem they wanted to work on. Initially, Caitlyn and Quentin thought they might work on a "cordless charger powered by solar cells." However, when they began discussing their observations, Quentin's comments about his specific family needs generated new insights for them. He had observed members of his family and his neighbors having a hard time with their electricity bills. Like many of their neighbors, his family had struggled to pay utility bills for years. For Quentin, reducing electric bills was an urgent and critical problem in his family life. Thus, when Caitlyn suggested the idea of a solar-powered cordless charger, he believed that his electric bills would "have a difference" if he used the charger at home.

Although the youth immediately liked the idea of a cordless charger powered by solar cells, they were able to appreciate the complexity of design decisions as they began leveraging the knowledge they had acquired from everyday experiences. While discussing possible design solutions, Quentin worried that the charger would not be very portable: "Should I carry the charger? Well, I think it is not convenient, because sometimes, I even forget to bring my cellphone to the school or the club. You think we can carry the charger, as well as your cellphone?" Quentin felt that carrying both a cellphone and a cordless charger could be inconvenient because he frequently forgot to bring his cellphone to school or the club. He also knew that this problem is not exclusive to him as he observed his peers having the problem.

Returning to their observations, the two noted that most of their friends, family, and neighbors also had cellphone cases. This led Caitlyn to suggest the idea of a *case* that was able to charge the cellphone using solar cells. Because a case always stays with its cellphone, people would not need to worry about forgetting to carry it. Quentin and the mentor said that this was a great idea, and the youth decided to develop it further. They settled on their possible solution: "a solar-powered cellphone case charger."

In another example, the "geodesic dome," we can further see how observational data led a group of girls to focus on trying to solve the problem of a lack of "play structures" specifically for their younger friends, as a particularly important community challenge. The club had one outdoor playground that could accommodate only a small number of children at a time. The youth talked about how "kids need to *move,*" and wished for more opportunities to be active during the hours they spent at the club. The youth had also observed, on different occasions, that since moving to new premises and with new furniture, the children were constantly reminded by club staff to be careful around the new items. These constant reminders led some of the youth to articulate that they "wish [they] were back at the old building where we can climb and sit anywhere." Building a dome that children could crawl into seemed like a fun and productive response. Upon observing how the younger club peers were indeed using the dome they had built for play and rest, Sasha, Ginny, and Tallie suggested additions to the dome to further the comfort and privacy of the children by making curtains and cushions and adding a rug. Finally, on observing the prominent location of the dome right by the lobby next to the entrance to the club, the youth decided that the dome needed to be further spruced up with galaxy-color spray paints.

Merging Epistemologies and Shared Ownership in Design

Youth makers need support in figuring out how to move from an idea to a working prototype, including how to build, evaluate, and optimize designs over several design cycles in ways that are responsive to community needs. Research indicates that *iterative* optimization is more effective in teaching design than a single design cycle (National Research Council, 2010). Most educational materials intended to support "designing solutions" focus broadly on the build-test-refine process, without attention to when or how multiple cycles take place, or what it means to work with data from different epistemological origins that may include conflicts, such as may happen when technical and social data are brought together. We are concerned with three dimensions of this process: (1) How do youth determine technical and social criteria (e.g., my scooter should be able to light up at night for at least 3 hours)? (2) How do youth balance competing factors (e.g., my energy requirements demand a bigger panel, but my friends want the scooter to look sleek and cool)? (3) How do students arrive at design trade-offs that enable real, testable, workable solutions?

The challenge here is in opening up the practice of STEM-rich projects. For example, youth may not initially realize that a solar-powered light-up scooter has specific energy requirements—based on the type/quantity of light desired, hours of power needed, or energy storage method—until they try a design with particular lights, solar panels, and power pack. They may not initially consider what kinds of light switches are easiest for small hands to use on-the-go, how sleek a design their peers may want, or what city/state ordinances might require of moving vehicles in the dark until they engage with various community members. In moving through design iterations these factors become more salient, but as they do, youth also need strategies for considering trade-offs as they further consider what design features are most affordable, important, and salient to their target audience. The goal is for their solutions to *actually work* for the people of *their community.*

Community dialogue and feedback cycles. We worked with youth to plan multiple feedback cycles with different community constituents throughout the design process, and coordinated these feedback sessions with different points in their design and prototyping cycles. The goal was to support youth in gaining access to different types of technical and/or social input that we thought could help them move their design work forward in incremental and realistic ways. This sometimes took on a more formal tone, as youth presented their projects to various stakeholders (e.g., local engineers, parents, community members, and peers) who provided written or oral feedback, or when youth involved various community members as prototype testers. Sometimes these feedback cycles were more informal, as various community members visited youth at their workstations and shared idea-generating conversations. In each of these approaches, youth engaged with a wide range of community members to understand their perspectives, and to leverage their expertise in ways that were deeply grounded in community toward their making projects.

For example, while the girls working on the SafePax (described earlier) tried different approaches to putting a working circuit together, they decided to conduct a second survey for more community feedback. They were concerned about how much money they might spend on their design. They wanted whatever they made to be easy to use, but they also wanted it to be affordable for their friends. Their new survey questions included: (1) Do you think the SafePax is a good idea for preventing bullying? Why? (2) How much would you pay for a SafePax? (3) What other features do you think the SafePax should have? This round of surveying brought data that suggested peers in the community thought it reasonable to pay $20 for a SafePax, but that $40 would be "too much."

After the girls had built a working circuit with littleBits, which were quite easy to use, Tonya asked one of the adult mentors how much the littleBits components cost. On learning the amount, Tonya loudly exclaimed, "That is TOO expensive! We can't use those for our project!! Nobody will be able to afford this bag!!" Lisa and Trina agreed that they had "a problem with the materials." With help from adult mentors, the girls researched online for more affordable materials, and had to investigate other ways of putting together their fairly complex circuit. They found that small plastic alarms with wires that could be connected into a circuit could be purchased for under $5. Together with the rest of the materials, they calculated that the final cost of building an alarm circuit would be under $15, including a solar panel that they would sew to the front of the backpack to keep a rechargeable battery charged, so as to continually power the alarm affordably. The girls were glad that they kept the materials of their prototype under $20, referring again to the community data they collected.

Keeping the materials of the backpack under the community indicated price of $20 was important to the three girls. Even though they had successfully built a prototype circuit with easy, snap-together electronics, the girls were determined to recreate the electronic component of their project with more affordable materials, on learning the cost of these parts. The social dimensions of their data—ensuring their bag would be affordable enough to meet the needs of the people for whom they are designing—drove the girls to reconsider the technical dimensions. The existing relationships the girls had with the youth and club staff members at the club provided them with easy and authentic access to community data that they trusted accurately reflected the particular contexts of their community. As a result, the girls significantly changed the makeup of their project.

Community dialogue and surveys/observations. Engaging in dialogue with community throughout the making process, from design phases through prototype testing phases, helped the youth continually develop their expertise as community ethnographers and makers while providing them with data points to advance their projects. Paying close attention to how their innovations are being received by the community also provided essential data points to the youth in subsequent iterative design.

The charging cellphone case. As Caitlyn and Quentin began to prototype their design, they initially decided to design a cellphone case for their own phones (both had the Samsung Galaxy 4) because the model was easily accessible to them for designing their Google SketchUp 3-D model (a graphical prototype). After designing their 3-D model based on the size and shape of their phones, the youth shared the model with peers and staff at their community club to get feedback about their design. However, as they talked with peers and staff around the club, they were immediately confronted with a new problem: Not many people in their community had the same phone they did.

Rather than working on a prototype that would work only for them, the two decided to design a survey to get more information on the kinds of phones used by their peers. Using an online-based survey-design program, they designed a 10-question survey focused on the following questions: What phones did people use? How important was it to charge on-the-go? Did they use a case? How long did their phone battery last?

Like the girls in the SafePax group discussed above, Caitlyn and Quentin conducted the survey among their peers and created multiple representations of their findings, including survey graphs and bubble maps of comments. They learned that most survey participants had an iPhone 5 and most used their phones more than 6 hours a day. They also learned that more than 90% of respondents valued the idea of "charging your phone on-the-go."

But the survey was not just about getting information; it was also about having conversations with the people they interviewed. The youth constructed their own lived scenarios to set up their survey: "You go to schedule an Uber and your phone dies, what do you do?"

Based on these data, Caitlyn and Quentin decided to revise their 3-D model for the iPhone 5 to benefit more people in their community. They could have served their own interests by designing for the Samsung Galaxy 4, but instead they chose to address the needs of the people in their community, based on the results of their survey (see Figure 4.2). They optimized their design to meet the special needs of their community and to further the public good.

Caitlyn and Quentin also wished to optimize their design by finding a way to help kids charge their phones during the school day. Most of their peers mentioned that their phones were out of power by the end of the school day without access to electrical outlets. However, Caitlyn raised the question of how effective a solar panel would be if it could not attract enough sunlight.

As they researched their ideas for a solar-powered cellphone case charger online, they discovered that a few cellphone cases powered by solar cells were already available, so they decided to investigate the pros and cons of these cases to figure out how to make their own design better. One of the things they found was that no solar-powered phone cases on the market at that time allowed the user to change the angle of the solar cells. Caitlyn and Quentin discussed why adjusting the angle of the solar cells was important:

> *Caitlyn:* The sun—it's in different spots.
> *Quentin:* Oh yeah, and during the time of day . . . so, it depends. At noon, this would be good, if we didn't move at noon, because at noon, it's right above you. But when it's the morning, this plays in this way. So the angle helps it.
> *Caitlyn:* So, your solar panel stays along with the sun.

The two youth understood that solar cells needed to be oriented toward the sun to draw the maximum amount of power and that the sun is "in different spots" during different times of the day. They said that they acquired this knowledge by engaging in a variety of maker club activities, such as taking fieldtrips to a solar-powered house and a solar panel array and making a solar-powered USB charger. Through these activities,

Figure 4.2. Survey Results ("What Kind of Phone Do You Have?")

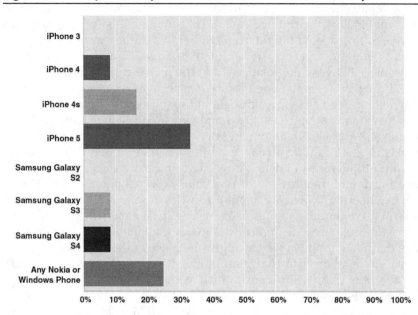

Caitlyn and Quentin had learned that power production depends on the angle of the solar cells. This knowledge led them to decide to make their solar-powered phone case in such a way that the user could adjust the angle of the solar cells.

Yet this presented a real problem for the two youth. They knew from their own experiences and that of their peers that if they fiddled with their phone in class it would be confiscated. They needed a "hands-free" design element that would enable kids to angle their solar panels toward windows in the classroom from their desks.

While discussing why adjusting the angle of the solar cells was important, Quentin raised another design issue with Caitlyn: "Okay, but if we put something on it, it will be harder to carry around. Maybe it will be hard to put it in my pocket." Quentin suggested simply leaning the phone case on something, like a wall, instead of revising their 3-D model to allow for adjustments to the angles of solar cells. Caitlyn agreed that it might be inconvenient to carry the phone case if they put something on it to adjust the angle of the solar cells, but she was not convinced that leaning the phone case on a wall was a good idea. She thought it would be hard to control the angle of the solar cells to draw the maximum amount of power and fully charge the cellphone.

After some discussion, Caitlyn suddenly mentioned the "door hinges" she had noticed in her house. She argued that the door hinges played a key role in adjusting the angle of rotation between a door and a wall and suggested adding a "hinge" piece between the solar cells and the phone case to enable users to control the angle of the solar cells. Caitlyn believed this would allow their phone case to collect enough power to charge an iPhone 5. Users could flip the panels down when they were carrying the phone. Quentin agreed to revise their 3-D model, and they drew the hinge piece between the solar cells and the phone case (see Figure 4.3).

Through integrating community perspectives by means of surveys, observations, and dialogues throughout the solar cell design process, Caitlyn and Quentin appreciated the complexity involved in making decisions to maximize design trade-offs in ways that attended to their responsibilities to the local and global communities. Caitlyn and Quentin drew upon multiple forms of data, knowledge, and experiences, including an investigation of the pros and cons of solar-powered phone cases, science and engineering knowledge about the angles of solar cells, and their own and their community's funds of knowledge and experiences. They considered multiple criteria and constraints as they optimized their designs. The youth had to find a way to adjust the angle of the solar cells in order to get enough power to charge an iPhone 5. Yet the issue of power was not the only criterion or constraint that they were considering at that moment. They were also trying to find a better way to meet the other criteria and constraints they had identified (e.g., the design of the phone case should not be bulky, as the case had to fit inside users' pockets or

Figure 4.3. Youth's 3-D Model of a Solar-Powered Phone Case

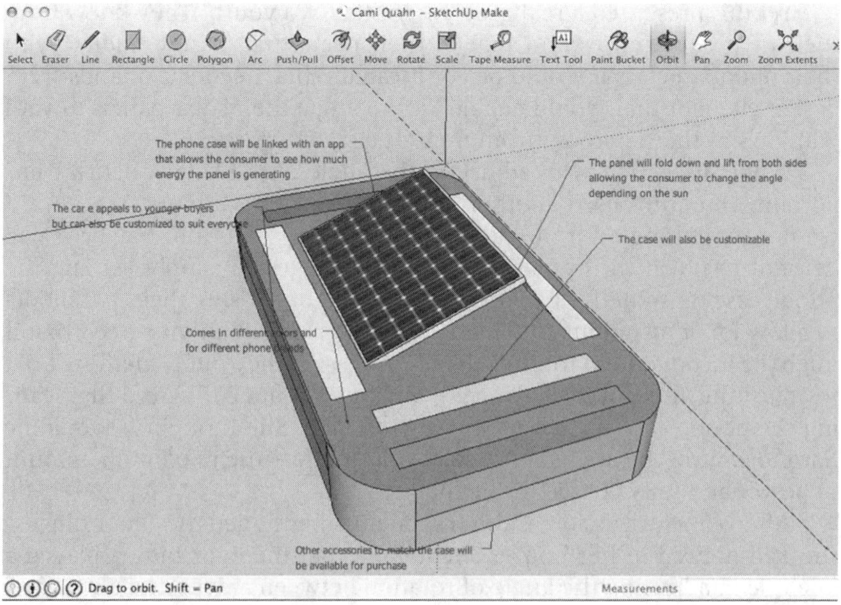

purses, and the solar cells should be angled so that users would not have to hold their phone awkwardly to collect sunlight). The youth felt responsible for finding a way to charge their phone fully on-the-go, in ways that were affordable and not bulky—approaches they felt were needed in their community but not addressed by cellphone makers. Their hybrid approach to the design solution—incorporating their technical expertise and their insights from community ethnography—reflects the complexity of the problem space they are working in.

Geodesic playdome. Another example of community perspectives affecting design is that of the geodesic playdome, which was reconstructed over time as the original makers plus new friends observed how it was being used in their club. When discussing the issue of how to help other children in the community, the youth brought up toys as a possibility, because "Kids don't have many toys," "We have no toys at the club that kids can play with," and "Maybe we can make toys to give to kids who are homeless, who just came here as refugees and who do not have toys."

Part of the initial process in deciding what kinds of toys they wanted to make included interviewing peers and adult mentors at the club, as well as online research. The youth spent time online and created Pinterest pages of ideas. While the youth searched online, Sharon was excited to find pictures of a geodesic playdome. She pinned several project ideas onto her Pinterest page. Ariel, a very shy 5th-grader, teamed up with Sharon for this project. They were immediately attracted to the idea of a dome for two different reasons. First, they were taken by the scale of the dome, and thought it would be "cool to build something so big." Second, they had observed the lack of play structures specifically for the younger children at their club, as well as the constant reminders by club staff to be careful around the new furniture, as described earlier. Once the dome was completed, the maker youth hosted a "Maker Toy Expo" at their club, where they introduced what they had made to the club community. They then set the dome out in the common area to see how other club peers might further interact with it. Upon observing how the younger club peers were indeed using the dome for play and rest, squeezing into the dome in twos and threes and poking their heads out of the window in turn, maker club youth Sasha, Ginny, and Tallie suggested additions to the dome to further the comfort and privacy of the children.

Building the initial dome was not easy. The girls had to work through challenging technical problems, such as how to make the proper-size triangles that would fit together for a secure dome, what materials they might use to construct the dome that were both affordable and durable, and where to have windows and doors so that the building was safe for little kids. Later, the two girls decided that it would be "cool to have lights inside the dome so kids can see because it's quite dark." They constructed

[handwritten margin note: ex of design iterations]

two paper circuits powered by solar panels that hung outside of the dome but whose wires wove into the circuit secured on the inside of the dome, that powered LED lights.

The geodesic dome (Figure 4.4) was impressive in size and drew much admiration from other youth makers and also other community members at the club. During a community event where the youth showcased their toys to the younger peers at the club, almost 30 younger children took turns crawling into the dome.

However, during the following summer, Ariel and Sharon were joined by three new members of the maker club (Sasha, Ginnie, and Tallie), and together they sought to modify the dome in significant ways. As the dome had become a part of everyday life at their community center, they began to notice several important things. First, they noticed that some of the younger children liked to take short naps in the dome. They also noticed that the children's naps were interrupted by people peeking through the windows, or because the children themselves were uncomfortable or cold. This led them to consider reworking the dome so that it had curtains for the window and doors ("for privacy and nobody be peeping in on you if you are taking a nap in there"). Using fabric and hot glue, the girls measured and cut out curtains, which they then glued onto the window and door of the dome. They then decided that a "rug" was necessary so that it would be "soft and cozy" inside the dome, since they had observed some of the smaller kids actually napping in the dome. Because they could not find a rug at the club, they made do with the largest piece of fabric from their making space supplies, which covered the required surface area. After they assembled the "rug" and created the curtains, the girls still felt that the dome was "not cozy enough." Sasha then suggested that she would sew cushions for the inside of the dome. She was very excited because, as she said, "I made the light-up cushion last summer for my project! I know how to do this and I can make some cushions for inside the dome!" Ginny and Tallie agreed that it was a good idea and they helped Sasha make two cushions for the dome.

Throughout the summer and into early fall, the geodesic playdome sat in a corner in the club lobby, utilized by many younger club children. Ms. Martha, one of the key staff members of the club, told us: "That dome is the most popular thing we've ever had at the club. It is amazing. ALL the kids just love it. They are just always crawling into it and playing and talking in there. Some of them even fall asleep in there. I just love it."

COMMUNITY ETHNOGRAPHY FOR EQUITABLE AND CONSEQUENTIAL MAKING

We believe that insights gleaned from the youth's stories in this chapter reveal how their making involves critical engagement with "the word

Figure 4.4. Geodesic Dome

and the world" (Freire, 1970) as community ethnography provided youth with the tools and space to explore and investigate local manifestations and experiences of particular systemic injustices. Across the phases of community ethnography, youth had opportunities to consider their own ideas against the background of their community's lived experiences, both challenges and the wisdom of lives lived. Engaging in community ethnography impacted what kinds of making youth did, with whom, for how long, using what materials, and to what ends. These are the everyday aspects that constitute the norms and practices of a making space, the shape of an emerging community making culture. As indicated by Table 4.1, the imbricating nature of shaping an emerging making culture while historicizing that very culture is an organic and continuous process, as youth engage in community ethnography. For example, the youth's intentions to "make for the common good" has led to them engaging in community-sharing events that range from making available their artifacts in a common space at the community club for other children to interact with to teaching workshops where youth makers plan, host, and teach other youth at the club how to make particular artifacts. Such an emerging culture informed by community ethnography is distinct from the dominant maker scene.

We recognize making as a historicized practice taking place across place and time, and community ethnography helps activate this ideal in ways that position youth as insiders to STEM-rich making. We believe

[handwritten margin note: ethnography impacted the type of making for how long; materials w/ whom]

Table 4.1. Summary of Community Ethnography Phases and Process

Community Data Collection Methods	Mapping the Problem Space		Merging Epistemologies and Practices
	Phase 1: Critical Engagement with Community to Frame the Issue	Phase 2a: Refining the Problem Space	Phase 2b: Designing Solutions Through Community Making
	Sustained Engagement Across Time and Space		
Surveys			
Interviews	• Please describe who you are: parent, kid, teenager, community member, teacher/staff • What are some challenges you face in your everyday life? • What are some challenges your community faces? • Can you tell me more about this challenge? How come people haven't been able to solve it? • How important is the issue of [fill in the challenge you identified here]? • Who do you think we should talk to for more information about who might be affected by this problem of interest?	• What do you think of this making idea that can address the challenge? • What do you think about the features of this product? Do you have any concerns and suggestions? [Related observation guidelines]	• How well does my prototype address the problem? In terms of functionality? In terms of cost? In terms of the user experience? • What other design features should be taken into consideration (technical) and why (social)? [Related observation guidelines]
Community Dialogues and Observations		• What are they doing? Who are they with? Where are they? • Who are they talking to? What are they saying? • Do you see them doing any hand gestures or body language that shows emotions? • How about eye contact?	• How are community members interacting with the prototype? How are they using it? • Are they using it in novel ways that you have not considered before? What does this mean for refining your design?
Purpose	To identify youth's own experiences with particular issue, collect data about community's experiences, make connections between these data to dig further into how community is experiencing this issue from multiple perspectives	To figure out what it means to be a community investigator in a space to innovate. What are the concrete making actions that youth can take that will address a homed-in dimension of the larger community issue already identified?	To engage in community-informed iterative making of prototype while considering trade-offs, balancing technical requirements with social specifications. To engage in testing of functionality of prototype
Illustrating Example	Samuel collecting community data to identify and unpack the different ways community members experience "unsafe streets"	Geodesic dome makers Ariel and Sharon focusing on a play structure large enough to encourage body movement of younger children	Caitlyn and Quentin switching phone model to prototype and incorporating a hinged solar panel to effectively capture sun rays

that youth's rootedness as insiders—and how that rootedness is translated through youth engaging in community ethnography as maker pedagogy into tangible knowledge and practices toward robust STEM-making that matters—is evidence of this. Here, we see the youth's movement of experiences into making—and dialogues on their making out into community—helps disrupt both local and sociohistorical narratives and practice (Cole, Kaptelinin, Nardi, & Vadeboncoeur, 2016).

LOOKING AHEAD

Across the narratives shared, there is evidence that community ethnography as pedagogy provided the youth with the tools they needed to engage in dialogue on the boundaries of making, and to engage in practices that challenged these boundaries. Youth navigated and challenged the boundaries that frame participation in making, such as expert/activist, insider/outsider, and community/STEM. These boundaries can reify historically situated claims to epistemic superiority (Lewis, 2012), such that when the public is brought into discussions on scientific or technical concerns, their views are considered outside of the technical realm (Roth, 2008). We also believe that community ethnography as pedagogy helped youth respond to and embody community narratives, as it is employed as a making practice in and of itself, rendering hybrid forms of STEM knowledge, practice, and tools in salient and accessible ways among a wider population and toward the social good. Here, the youth's systemic integration of ethnographic data positioned youth as experts on obtaining and interpreting community knowledge. It also positioned community knowledge as an integral part of technical design. The process of generating community ethnographic data and integrating them into STEM-rich making is a dialogic. That is, as the youth sought to learn with members of their community about their experiences, they also shared their ideas about and access to STEM-rich making with members of community, further challenging boundaries of making. This dialogic stance is a way the youth and community respond to and challenge established power dynamics.

Community ethnography should be dialogic (dialogue between youth & community)

CHAPTER 5

Co-Making
Imagining New Social Futures Through Community Making

> When you are engineering, when you are making your invention, first of all, you have to talk to people. You have to interview people in your community. You might know what the problems are, but you might not know how it matters to other people. You have to figure out how other people care, and you have to get their ideas, and learn what they know. . . . When we made our library, we had to figure out what we needed to make it. We needed to know where it would go, what it could look like, and stuff we put in it. We had our ideas, but our ideas weren't enough. —Samuel, 14-year-old maker

Samuel shared this quote with us about his efforts to build a "Little Free STEM Library" with his friend, Fall, while working in a making space at their local community center over a 2-year period. His quote highlights how important it is for young people to be able to have opportunities to make in collaboration with others. He wanted to point out that his community had important ideas that contributed greatly to his Little Free STEM Library project. He and his friend made the library so that the children at their club could have free and unfettered access to science books and mini-maker kits—things they knew, from experience and surveys of community members, were not easily available in his community. They also added blinking LED lights around the library, powered initially by a hand crank generator and later by a solar panel, to call attention to the library, and to get kids curious about how the circuit worked.

In Chapter 4, we examined how community ethnography supported youth in building a more equitable culture of making—in how they were able to break down critical power dynamics and leverage cultural knowledge and practice alongside STEM in powerful ways. In this chapter we extend this discussion to further examine how integrating community ethnography as pedagogy also supports an equity-oriented culture of making by promoting the practice of co-making.

In the quote above, Samuel framed the importance of sustained engagement with his community as a part of making. He points out that by interviewing and talking with different people in his community he was able see the problems he cared about in new ways. He also viewed his engagement with community as shaping the outcomes of his work. He needed to know where to put the finished library so that it would be accessible to others. His idea for including the maker kits was also inspired by observing how much the younger children enjoyed sneaking into the making space to play with the paper circuit materials. Aligning with Samuel's comments, this chapter on co-making is not just about the involvement of different people in the process, although that is important. Rather, co-making involves the inclusion of multiple perspectives, putting different planes of knowledge and experience on a shared level.

SUPPORTING A CULTURE OF CO-MAKING

The idea of co-making has been central to the maker movement through its embrace of participatory culture. Jenkins (2006) describes a participatory culture as "a culture with relatively low barriers to artistic expression and civic engagement, strong support for creating and sharing creations, and some type of informal mentorship whereby experienced participants pass along knowledge to novices" (p. 3). Grounded in social constructionist views of learning, a participatory culture focuses on the "whole student" as a "citizen in a rich eco-system" where learning happens as students move through experiences in school, after-school, home and online, integrating and re-mixing ideas, tools, and resources. Participatory culture is a potentially powerful way to consider the possibilities of maker learning because of its focus on movement and connections. A participatory culture potentially supports beginning makers in contributing to and feeling socially connected with other makers, where the activities they engage together are relevant to their interests and identities (Alper, Hourcade, & Gilutz, 2012). It also positions makers as active cocreators rather than consumers of ideas (Kafai, Peppler, & Chapman, 2009).

Yet, power and positioning have not been taken up as core concerns in what a participatory culture may mean. When the youth visited makerspaces at local universities, libraries, and membership-paying making spaces in their cities, as discussed in Chapter 3, they were impressed by the sophisticated making tools and the possibilities for making projects. However, they were equally firm in their refusal of particular aspects of these making spaces, when it came to designing their own. In youth parlance, they noted that these spaces they visited were "not kid-friendly," occupied by "mostly White adults," and "had many things we can't touch." One youth said that she did not feel as if "[she] was wanted there." When asked what they would like their community making space to be like, youth offered up visions where "you can spill your

definition of participatory culture

ideas with no judgment," and where "nobody be telling you that you can't do that when they don't even know you," where they can "make for good."

Others have been critical of this point as well. It has been argued that makerspaces can advance participatory culture by serving as "sites that shape new civic identities through cultural practices" (Shea, 2016, p. 232)—a sort of *"DIY citizenship"* (Ratto & Boler, 2014), where the process of making reflects how "we build ourselves, our cultures, and our institutions through processes of material engagement" (Ratto, 2011, p. 253). Ratto uses the term *critical making* to refer to the kind of making that merges social insights with engineering design (Ratto, 2011), such as using cost-effective 3-D printing of prostheses for use in the developing world (Schmidt, Chen, Gmeiner, & Ratto, 2015).

A participatory culture of critical making emphasizes the "praxis-oriented" activities and energies of the *collective* (Ratto, 2011, p. 253). This is especially relevant to our work. We, too, are concerned with supporting the youth's agency to make in ways that have consequential outcomes for themselves and their communities, collaborating with youth to figure out what a community-based, youth-driven making space entails structurally, culturally, and practically. We are further concerned with the ways in which the emergent culture also promotes a maker culture that pushes back against intersecting injustices in their maker clubs and communities as well as in the worlds of STEM and making.

Furthermore, although people may be invited to participate in a makerspace, how their participation transforms that place for themselves and others has not been a part of this equation. This concern is at the heart of the equity agenda in making. Without access to ideas and tools and a space to make, one is left out of the movement; yet the spaces, tools, and ideas as currently constructed in-practice may themselves act as high-barrier atmospheric walls even if one has physical access to the space (Vrasti & Dayal, 2016).

Thus, rather than focus on participatory culture, we use the term *co-making* to draw attention to norms and routines that create spaces for and help legitimize input from many different people across time and settings. This includes youth codeveloping criteria for making projects/progress, valuing student and community members' input toward shaping project process and outcomes, encouraging project work to occur in many different places drawing upon the resources in the places, spending large chunks of time on supporting youth in negotiating their own ideas with others, and sharing ownership of the making process and project. There is no maker playbook for what constitutes community-engaged participatory culture in making for youth from nondominant communities. Who are the mentors in these spaces? What kinds of knowledge would they pass on, and to whom? What are the kinds of supports necessary for creating

ways co-making is used [handwritten margin note]

and sharing innovations (and in what ways), especially within the communities that matter to the youth?

In this chapter, we share three main claims about co-making. First, we describe how community ethnography enabled and supported a practice of co-making. Second, we examine how co-making through community ethnography contributed to more porous boundaries—the greater movement of ideas, people, tools, and resources. This offered youth expanding opportunities to grow their social networks, and to gain recognition for their efforts across communities of practice. Third, we discuss how co-making helped reorganize traditional knowledge/power hierarchies in ways that still supported youth's development in robust, project-relevant STEM knowledge, challenging views of what it means to be an expert STEM-rich maker.

How Community Ethnography Enables and Supports a Practice of Co-Making

Ethnographic tools are employed by educators and youth as part of the making process in order to engage with community. Tools such as dialogic and structured interviews with community members, observations, and member checking and feedback on project development made movement of project ideas, resources, and stakeholders possible. The youth's project work took place in the making space *and* in various community spaces, through utilizing ethnographic tools such as surveys, conversations, interviews, and observations (e.g., while waiting for the bus in the cold, playing at the playground, walking to school, with friends on the basketball court, with parents, siblings, and grandparents), as much as through actual movement of the physical making (e.g., testing prototypes in real community spaces, bringing in duct tape prototypes made at home, etc.). This movement of project work enabled youth to more directly leverage a wider range of knowledge and practice toward their making projects. This we view as an important form of movement, in that as youth talked with community members and brought their critiques to bear on their projects they also moved *ideas* about their making from one space to another, in equitable and consequential ways. This pushes beyond leveraging existing funds of knowledge in two ways. One, as the youth seek to directly ground their work in multiple systems of relationality incrementally, previously distal threads of insider knowledge gain currency as funds of knowledge now relevant to informing youth's making design. Second, we see how different threads of funds of knowledge intersect to provide youth with multiple perspectives that impact making design trade-offs. For example, these ethnographic tools assisted youth in recognizing those problems as part of broader, entrenched challenges that their community members had struggled with or negotiated over time.

co-making leads to movement of projects both dialogically + physically (testing design in community)

Community dialogue was essential, for example, in supporting one group of youth understanding problems of homelessness with more complexity and nuance than is easily reached without such person-to-person interaction. The Donator app group had initially approached the problem space of homelessness as a one-dimensional issue focused on providing specific resources to individuals in need. Well-intentioned, some group members had a limited understanding of actual people's stories, concerns, and tensions, even though they had peers in the program who had been homeless. Interviews with one maker educator who had experienced homelessness herself, and also with housing campaign organizers and homeless shelter directors, helped Donator app designers Zani and Luca develop a more multifaceted, more tangible, and more human understanding of what it means to be homeless at the individual and systemic level. Here we see the girls' efforts to visit homeless centers, talk to friends and staff who are or had been homeless, and investigate the issue online, as a way to move and coalesce ideas across spaces in ways that transformed their own views and their projects. As a result, the girls began to discuss the issue in terms of housing rights at national, state, city, and individual levels, and they explored how they could leverage their own experiences with both housing resources and digital technologies to engineer a potential solution. Zani and Luca connected what they learned from their interviews and research to a simulation game they played on their phones, inspiring their design of an app that would not only connect users to volunteering and donation information, but would also take users through the lives of individuals who had experienced homelessness. Through their use of critical ethnographic research tools, the girls transformed their own knowledge of their problem space and moved their community-informed knowledge outward to other spaces to educate and empower other community members as fellow housing rights allies.

A second example shows the importance of making educators reweaving community and family perspectives back into projects. When Jennifer and Emily got "stuck" on how to design a non-bulky heated jacket, one of their maker educators reminded them of a funny video diary they made earlier on insulation, and she suggested that they go back and watch it to get some ideas. The girls watched and laughed at their video, breaking down tensions that surfaced at the frustrations of their project. The video involved a reflection on Jennifer's experiences at home with their fireplace and the insulation her father had put around it. The fireplace became central the previous winter when their home was without electricity for 2 weeks because of a powerful winter storm. She explained, "When we had that big snowstorm here and everyone's power went out. The silver lining, I seen a lot of it, because we had to put it in our fireplace. We had to put silver lining around it so the heat would stay in it, but it wouldn't burn anything outside of it." Jennifer and Emily asked us if we could get them some "silver lining" material to help them try to "keep the jacket warm" with smaller and less bulky heating elements.

In a third example, we see how conversations at home led to parental expertise that shaped youth's and their peers' experiences in making. Peter and Kalvin wished to help elderly, wheelchair-bound babysitters. Both boys had extensive experience with babysitting responsibilities and Peter knew of elderly caregivers who had difficulty manipulating tension baby gates. The two boys sought to hack an ordinary baby gate to make it motion sensor–activated. The project was fairly complex, and required expertise not possessed by either the youth or the making educators. When confronted with the challenge of being unsure of how to proceed, Peter suggested that his father might be able to help. Peter's father, a carpentry expert, shared advice on how to take apart a tension baby gate using particular tools that will retain the integrity of both gate panels. A local maker educator also visited to learn how to mechanically hack the gate, and then, in turn, showed the boys how to consider different ways to mobilize one panel, while keeping the other fixed, during a community feedback session. With these inputs the boys were able to spend extensive time testing different mechanisms with different-sized motors, fishing line, LEGO blocks, and wheels, before a prototype with a moving panel on wheels was completed after 6 months of work.

In each of these cases, maker educators resisted telling youth how to proceed from a solely making standpoint, but instead sought outside community resources to support youth in refining their design problem-space—returning to video diaries, valuing basketball time and visits by friends, and inviting parents, physically and through story, into the space. These were made possible because the design process enacted in these spaces asked youth to seek ongoing input from community at each stage in their making process. Through co-making, the youth had new ways to see, use, and legitimize the wisdom and the funds of knowledge of their community.

In the above examples, we see how community ethnography allowed for different people and practices to bring in new tools and community wisdom and funds of knowledge for negotiating and rewriting injustice through youth's STEM-rich making. The inclusion of new people and practices through the making process further supported the youth in iteratively refining their problem space and project ideas toward greater responsiveness to their communities.

In their projects, several youth indicated that their designs were inspired by people and events in their lives. Youth acknowledged that these people and events sometimes gave them initial project ideas—as we saw with the interviews and surveys providing inspiration for the light-up football, the heated jacket, and the light-up umbrella, to name a few. Honing their making design through community ethnography also helped surface relevant gaps in the making and STEM knowledges, which maker-mentors helped address through what we call just-in-time (JiT) STEM or making how-to activities. For example, the JiT activities Samuel engaged in while designing and making his light-up football included learning about circuits, kinds of circuits, and calculating energy requirements to power a specific load. Youth also acknowledged that wide community input during the initial prototyping process led them to take new directions in their work, and changed how they thought about who owned the project and the range of expertise they needed to develop.

For example, the Timmy project shifted from a heated shoe thought up by two boys to a light-up heated boot created by, at one point or another, 12 boys (three lead boys and nine "drop-in" peers). As one of the lead boys stated, "At first, we were going to make a heated shoe 'cuz [our teacher] has a broken ankle and we did not want her toes to get cold." However, they changed their project so that at the end, "The Timmy is for people that can't afford shoes, people that don't have boots for winter, like homeless people that we see in [our] city. Our product is very useful for winter and for people that have cold feet, or just want to look cool. And we'll be coming out with heated or cooling house slippers to keep you warm or cool depending on the time of the year."

The Timmy, a Timberland® boot outfitted with heating elements on the interior soles, LED tube lights around the outer sole, and powered by rechargeable batteries hidden in the tongue of the boot, took the boys 6 months to successfully prototype. The project first began to take its new direction when Maken and Tel would leave their maker club after only about 30 minutes of work to play basketball. (It was the only time in the evening that the court at the community club was open to free play.) When they played ball, they talked about their project, and their basketball mates would follow them back to the maker club after free court time was over. We noticed that the visiting friends would help with some tasks, often calling out and laughing with impossible scenarios for the boys to consider: What about if you miss the bus and have to walk to school? What if you really need them but you can't pay for them? This engagement with peers outside the making program slowed the group's work down significantly, but it also led to design considerations that advanced the boot toward better addressing the needs of their peers: fashion, affordability, and comfort. The two boys (and one friend who officially joined the project) were asked to modify their design sketch to include these new ideas, labeling them under new inputs for "technical" and "social" considerations. This sketch provided an important space as it allowed the boys and their making educators to return to conversations about how to address these new concerns. JiT activities the Timmy youth makers explored that were informed by these criteria included testing energy requirements of different heating elements and the science behind energy transformations.

We also point out that one of the making educators felt that Maken's departure from the making program after 30 minutes to play ball was a distraction to other youth. However, another teacher noticed that his basketball playing opened a pathway for him to share his work with his peers, bringing them into the club. Such tensions of making sense of how youth author novel pathways to co-making (potentially seen as disruptive) are powerful if validated, and have implications for seeding an emergent making culture at the community club.

Youth also linked racial and gender injustice with the challenge of gaining legitimacy in making. James and Megan designed "Do-It-Yourself Green Energy" (DIG) videos on using green energy sources for making projects, such as solar panels and piezo pads (small pads that convert vibrational energy to electric energy). Their idea for this project grew out of their frustration with not finding useful information on how to use piezo pads online. As Megan explains, "I have been thinking about this for the last 2 years, since I really first started to come to [the maker program]. The problem was that we had to read materials [online] written for adults. Some students will not have a problem reading but some will. We eventually got [our project] to work, but it took a lot of extra time. It would help if we had materials that were kid-friendly." Megan's understanding of the culture of making grew out of her participation over 2.5 *years*. After experiencing "too many times" when she could not find makers like herself on the Internet, she decided to do something about it with James.

As Megan and James interviewed other youth in community about the problems they identified, they expanded their rationale to address new related scales of concern: the stereotyping of people like them (girls of all ethnicities and African Americans) in STEM. As they stated in their project description, "Also people say that African Americans and girls, it doesn't matter your race, are not interested in STEM. Did it surprise us that most of the videos we did find were done by White men? Not really. That is great, but we wanted to see videos made by people like us. We also want to show people like us that we can do this work, too. Our videos will be made available free on the [maker program] YouTube station." They also noted the lack of STEM resources for people in their community to do STEM because of local economies and practices. As James wrote, "In [the city] there are not many after-school STEM programs, and definitely not many kid-friendly makerspaces. Where will kids learn these skills? In our videos, of course!"

Here, we further emphasize the importance of longitudinal participation in identifying intersectional experiences of injustice within making and to which making can respond. If Megan had not participated over years, she may not have identified a pattern, but rather accepted the reality as is. Having time and the tools to see and reflect on these challenges mattered. Most youth did not begin their design work with these inter-secting ideas in mind. Many youth, at first, were not sure of what project to work on. Over months, their participation in surveying community members supported them in noticing which concerns were most salient, where, when, and for whom. Though these connections were not made solely through these surveys, the approach created the space for new questions to be opened and new discourses to be legitimized, among both youth and teachers. The ensuing multivoiced perspectives allowed youth to identify and name injustices that they might previously have accepted as the norm, such as how public libraries have rules that disproportion-ately marginalize low-income youth, a data point that inspired Samuel to build the Little Free STEM Library with his friend Fall.

Co-Making Led to More Porous Boundaries Toward Expanding Opportunities to Be Recognized

That the "walls" between the making program and the youth's worlds appeared to grow more porous is an important aspect of the develop-ing culture of their making spaces. Porous boundaries mean that peo-ple, ideas, and resources flow more easily between the making space and other worlds, and that nontraditional knowledge and practice (funds of knowledge) are valued in the making space, alongside relevant STEM knowledges that are picked up through just-in-time activities. We believe these points are substantiated in the two previous sections. Here, we fo-cus more on how these porous boundaries provided opportunities to be recognized for one's developing STEM-rich making expertise.

When Chris brought his anti-bully app (which included a crowd-sourcing component to layer on new data inputs from users) to school to show his science teacher, she asked him to present his idea to the class. He told the students he made his app so that they (and others) could contribute to it: "It won't work good unless you add to it." When he did so, his peers exclaimed at how important his project was; they declared he was "changing the world," "would be famous," and asked, "Why can't we do stuff like that here [in school]?" This short interaction brought on by connecting Chris's out-of-school STEM-rich making with Chris's in-school science activities gained Chris more formal recognition from teacher and classmates while also showing his science teacher pos-sibilities in looking across spaces in youth's STEM experiences. When Samuel brought his phantom jacket to school to show his science class, an activity scaffolded by his making educators, his friend Darrin walked to the front of the room with him to help him demonstrate because he "helped to make the jacket, too." Darrin had stopped into the club mak-ing space a few times to mess around with Samuel and gave ideas on where to put the phantom image on the jacket and where to place the shoulder turbines. After the class visit, and Samuel and Darrin's newly shared recognition, the two boys began to plan new projects together, and Darrin attended more regularly until his family moved to a new city.

Second, we point out that the locations of porous boundaries fostered by co-making led youth to increase movement of people and the maker projects, fostering shared project ownership. This is evident in the two examples above, but is particularly visible in how Kairee and Jaida resolved some tensions they encountered as they worked on their Heated Bus System. The girls could not decide whether to heat the bus seats or the bus stop. Jaida insisted on making the seats in the buses warmer—"My mom always gets cold when the bus door opens to let people in." Kairee wanted to make the bus shelters warmer—"bus stops are cold." As they rode the bus, they surveyed people both waiting and riding the bus. They took careful notes of the number of bus shelters on their route and their condition, the number of seats on each bus and their condition, and the concerns that riders had. They also talked to people who did not ride the bus and tried to figure out if their project ideas would encourage them to start riding. As Jaida explained: "There are 53 seats on every standard bus. . . . Not only that, but several people who do not currently ride the bus told us that they would be interested in riding the bus if they knew that the bus came equipped with heated seats. We know this from a survey that we took around our neighborhoods."

Through this ethnographic process, they began to see their project as having two connected parts, addressing the needs of the whole community, not just the people who currently rode the bus. At the same time, by having their ideas expanded about project ownership by involving many different community members, they found themselves with more challenging technical considerations to solve, which necessitated more JiT STEM activities. They began to see, for example, that a heated bus stop should be accessible to a wide range of riders with different physical abilities and needs. Kairee suggested that the system should include "high-wattage halogen lamps" to heat the bus stop while also including "surface heating elements like a heating pad" on the bus shelter's bench. Porous boundaries between the youth's salient but previously less connected communities—school, community maker club, different community spaces—led to increased recognition of youth's expanding making expertise even as the mobility of resources between these spaces enhanced youth's making designs in increasingly complex ways. Porous boundaries also serve to increase the consequentiality of youth's making, when youth appreciate the interconnected ways and different arenas in their lives that their making projects may simultaneously impact. Additionally, porous boundaries between community knowledge and STEM knowledge in the form of related JiT activities supported youth in developing robust STEM knowledge in the context of community making that is immediately applicable to their purposes.

Co-Making Reorganized Traditional Knowledge/Power Hierarchies

Welcoming new and diverse perspectives as a part of design allowed new opportunities and structures for youth to be recognized for their experiences and relationships. The previous examples illustrate maker educators becoming co-learners alongside youth as outsiders provided help and insight at critical moments. It is important that forms of community and family funds of knowledge served to resolve both complex technical problems as well as social design elements. When Peter's father helped the boys hack the baby gate, it opened possibilities for JiT STEM activities, testing motors not previously thought structurally possible. When Samuel's mother argued strongly for Nerf material for his football, it made locating the batteries at the ball's center of gravity a solvable problem. When the basketball friends who helped with the Timmy demanded that the shoe be stylish, comfortable, and affordable, the group had to reconsider types of heating elements and battery storage, necessitating more JiT activities that the boys were keen to engage in.

Yet youth's making was valued for both the technical quality of their innovations and for how their lives were deeply ensconced as an integral part of their design. Having multiple forms of expertise and ways to enact these toward solving injustices were both a process and product of co-making. As one teacher, who had been working with youth for 4 years stated, "In spending time in youth-owned spaces, I have changed as a person who is now more aware and more awakened to how little I know and how much I can learn from youth." Another teacher stated, "I first worried that the girls were being so loud and disruptive as they ran in and out of the club room. Then I realized that the lobby was a major social space, and their movement got other kids asking them about what they were spending all their time on. I had to begin to see that movement is essential in the girls being girls *and* being makers." These quotes illustrate how co-making can support multiple perspectives, as well as flatten power dynamics.

Lastly, while maker educators may hold deep knowledge of some practices and ideas needed for the youth's making designs to be successful, they did not always have the same depth of community knowledge or specialized applications to help youth solve particular problems. Youth took note of their maker educators' need for their expertise in guiding them forward. As Zae noted: "At first, I didn't really know what [the maker club] was. I got it mixed up with [robotics club]. And so I said I was going to join robotics. Which, in robotics we had to follow instructions on how to build things and in [our maker club] we actually have to change the instructions a little bit . . . 'cuz they [maker educators] wouldn't know how to do it without us."

CO-MAKING TOWARD NEW RELATIONALITIES IN MAKING

Community ethnography as a part of STEM-rich making promoted equity-oriented outcomes through helping make visible community wisdom and funds of knowledge as sources of disruption of historicized injustice toward a practice of co-making. Anchored in co-making, this maker culture reflects youth's values and desires—making toward a more just world. Such a culture legitimately repositions community wisdom and funds of knowledge as sources of making and spaces within which to make. It also makes possible new opportunities to leverage STEM knowledge and practice alongside community wisdom and funds of knowledge as maneuverable hybrid tools for pushing back against the injustices youth hope to solve.

In this section, we extend our discussion of co-making to consider how the kinds of co-making made possible through community ethnography are relational activities, involving processes that can bring together many different people and perspectives through greater movement and disrupting powered boundaries. Making intersects with systemic forces through sanctioned power hierarchies and practices. This view emphasizes that making always takes place in spaces and times influenced by institutional, societal, and individual histories. It also emphasizes how making involves the process of reauthoring and re-mixing practices from a wide range of experiences, located in the home, community, and school, among other places, toward reorienting social relations and knowledge hierarchies.

Here, given our focus on culture, we explicitly invoke an anthropological view of relationality (Eckert, 2016), where relationality asserts both interconnectedness and difference through how we all subjectively construct ourselves and the other. Focused on more than vertical movement (e.g., such as novice to expert), this dynamic and critical view illuminates the ways in which learning takes shape in how people, ideas, tools, resources, bodies, and relationships move and remix as people engage in social practice toward new futures. New forms of hybrid knowledge and practice arise as people move horizontally, from place to place, widening what counts as expertise by including "the negotiation of various contexts and the development of hybrid solutions" (Vossoughi & Gutiérrez, 2014, p. 610).

More recently, DiGiacomo and Gutiérrez (2016) have advanced this work to consider the importance of relational equity in making and tinkering. As we reflect on these ways in which community engagement

[handwritten margin note: Community engagement, support, co-making]

supports youth in STEM-rich co-making, we begin to see the salience of relationality in fostering a culture of making that is equitably consequential. The previous literature on cultural views of learning and human development calls attention to the importance of relationality, in terms of the ways in which learning takes shape in how people, ideas, tools, resources, and bodies move and re-mix across time and space as people engage in social practice toward new futures. We found this to be true in our study as well.

However, our findings suggest that we need to further consider the ways in which relationality matters, particularly toward transformative ends. We are concerned with how relationality attends to transformation of the structures that define and constrain relationships (such as power dynamics, boundaries, and geographical proximities), the kinds of access to resources, activities, and tools bound to particular relationships, and how relationships can shift as these resources, activities, and tools shift. We see these forms of relationality supporting an expanding maker culture with opportunities for co-constructing new spaces to imagine new social futures. However, tensions also arise as a part of this. We discuss these points below.

Expanding a Maker Culture

The youth's practice of co-making was geared toward relationality. That *[handwritten margin note: def. of relationality]* is, the youth's making practices were grounded in their own locations in the world as youth growing up in historically marginalized communities, but with broad cultural wealth and a hope for using their making work to advance their communities. We view such relationality as critical, in the sense that the youth leveraged their sustained making work to heighten *[handwritten margin note: use making to heighten awareness of injustice]* their own and others' awareness and understandings of intersectional experiences of injustice. We also view such relationality as connected, in terms of how youth were related to the issues they were investigating, to other youth involved in the project, to community members they interviewed, and to adult mentors, as well as to the broader systems of power that shape their experiences in the world as young people of color growing up in lower-income communities. Such relationality also attends to the intersectionality (Crenshaw, 1991) between youth's lives across spaces.

The youth's co-making practices involved mobilizing the knowledge and relationships, from across the spaces of their lives, into their making as essential for advancing their STEM work. In so doing, youth relied on their relationships with peers and adults to define the making problem with more clarity, and engaged in ongoing dialogue with community members and making educators to finesse their projects. This integration of community knowledge and practice with STEM making was viewed as necessary for projects to be successful. Here, the role of digging more deeply into STEM took on local significance rather than reflecting a school and/or White male culture, reflecting modes of dynamic learning (Leander, Phillips, & Taylor, 2010) and intersectionality (Unterhalter, 2012).

We saw this in how Jaida and Kairee described what they needed to know to make their "bus warming system" work for all riders, in the specific content of the DIY videos made by Megan and James, and in the weeks-long struggle to figure out the correct power requirements for a solar-powered heated jacket, among others. In our findings, we illustrated how this promoted the practice of co-making. Here, we see co-making not only shifting the culture of making toward legitimizing multiple forms of expertise and spaces of making, but also foregrounding the urgency of making toward justice-oriented ends. *[handwritten: relationality large part of co-making as most problems emerged from your histories]*

This shift toward relationality as a framing cultural dimension is important, because it requires consideration of how youth sought to transform relations among youth makers, the content and practice of making, and their making peers, teachers, and community toward who they are and want to be (both individually and collectively), and the possibilities for their making work (Engeström & Sannino, 2010). The problems youth sought to address *emerged from their locations and histories, rather than from the interest* of any given individual. When youth such as Samuel (light-up football) or Jennifer and Emily (light-up scooter) gathered data about the length of days in their northern-city location, the locations of non-working streetlights in their community, or how their friends kept out of trouble after school, these community data all contributed to their project designs. We see here how such relationality is not purely social, but also grounded within geo-historical dimensions regarding length of days and urban infrastructure. As these projects made visible such forms of relationality, they also became resources to build on, and bridges to connect to relevant STEM knowledges (JiT). Such expanding relationality legitimized the possibilities for broader purposes and goals in making, and in the social and materials resources that could be used in making.

In particular, the design approach leveraged within these two making spaces grounded in community engagement offered youth opportunities to build relationality into their making culture. Building relationality into making, by leveraging tools of community ethnography to support community engagement, further *legitimized* movement of ideas and resources from one space to another as a necessary part of making. Community engagement offered youth a way to see and understand their own relationality—that is, how youth are related to the issue they are investigating, to other youth involved in the project, to community members they interview, and to adult mentors, as well as to the broader systems of power that shape their experiences in the world as young people of color growing up in lower-income communities. They had multiple opportunities to see patterns of concern within their community that further offer questions to help them seek and reinforce relevance to their communities. They could see the social, political, and ethical dimensions of the problems and solutions they hope to tackle, as well as the importance of their work toward community development.

This view is more than access and opportunity to making (e.g., Martin, 2015), and more than recognizing other ways of knowing, or experiences in the worlds of making (e.g., Peppler & Bender, 2013), where most equity-oriented attention is paid. This view has a disruptive dimension that focuses on challenging historicized inequalities as a part of making.

The implication that follows suggests that how youth makers are supported to examine their concerns (nested within broader community considerations) shapes not only their development as makers, but also the making culture. This intersecting approach reframes making both in terms of process and outcome. This culture supports the deliberate departure from predesigned making activities (e.g., make a robot that draws for you with these materials) redolent of the "keychain" syndrome (Blikstein & Worsley, 2016) previously described so as to best support making projects that authentically contribute to the improvement of conditions for youth. Furthermore, this culture supported deeper engagement in STEM knowledge and practice through JiT activities, when community perspectives or needs demanded more robust designs. When the Timmy (heated light-up boot) was not comfortable, the youth makers needed to revise their heating element design, a particularly complex technical challenge.

Expanding Social Futures

Few studies deeply consider what undergirds youth making, especially as it relates to their social futures. Yet the youth's critical engagement with community is apparent in the issues they chose to tackle—for example, bullying and the higher risk of rape in the more vulnerable populations in which our youth have membership. Through the collaborative nature of their co-making (from recruiting the help of outside peers who are experts in the issues at hand to soliciting help from expert family members who do not necessarily recognize themselves as "makers" but who nonetheless possess relevant making expertise, such as sewing and carpentry), youth challenged the notion of who can be named a maker. They broadened the boundaries of a "local maker community" to include salient others who might not be tapped as germane resources in a typical STEM-focused maker program.

By engaging with community as part of their making practices, the youth placed new attention on making as a process not just of producing new artifacts, but also of co-constructing *new spaces for imagining new social futures* (DiGiacomo & Gutiérrez, 2016). Such space-making involves re-narrating past experiences and projecting new futures where they are powerful producers and critics of STEM and their worlds. This work was made possible by dialogue fostered by engaging making with community, in response to injustices faced by community. We believe this approach fundamentally departs from previous work on facilitation in making in its attention to how making *maps onto lives, relationships, and spaces over time.*

We also suggest that making itself, when fostered through community engagement, more than being responsive to community needs, further reifies those needs for others to acknowledge, while presenting directionality toward the future. This matters now, more than ever, when historical injustices have been pushed to the side as individual attributes in need of remediation.

Jurow and Shea (2015) remind us that understanding what matters to people requires us to make sense of how their lives are shaped by and shape social and institutional practices, and within that, the possibilities for imagining new forms of life. In terms of the youth's making practices and projects, we see how their work required attention to both social and spatial scales of injustice, that when addressed through an ever-expanding network of co-making, created a greater possibility for collectively organized and valued social futures (Jurow & Shea, 2015).

The youth in this study engaged in expansive forms of making that enabled them "to become designers of their own social futures" (Gutiérrez, 2008, p. 156). We believe that emphasizing relationality in making spaces means acknowledging youth as individuals with concerns grounded in location and history, but also with the agency to act. When youth and making educators engaged in conversation around problem definition and solution design, youth were encouraged to present as many perspectives and relevant points of view as they deemed significant. As a further move to transform the maker culture to co-making with youth, the maker educators began to work toward deliberate mindfulness in keeping the relationality focus in these dialogues, which helped attend to inclusivity and sought to broaden perspectives. Youth held very different ideas about what mattered in the community from one another, and from what maker educators anticipated. By soliciting for and validating youth's varying nodes of relationality, maker educators were able to support youth's agency in framing the community safety problem space for themselves. Instead of responding to parameters laid out by their teachers, the youth, through community ethnography, framed salient safety issues for themselves to investigate and innovate.

With consequential and equity-oriented making as their object, youth leveraged everyday and STEM knowledge, from a variety of sources and in many different forms, making possible incremental movement toward new imagined futures for themselves and their communities. In these new imagined futures, youth have a voice and place in STEM, and their communities enact power toward social transformations. These futures are nonreductive, grounded in the idea that change in the individual involves change in the social situation itself.

NEGOTIATING TENSIONS INHERENT IN RELATIONALITY AND CO-MAKING

There were tensions, often profound, that pushed back on the more expansive forms of relationality that undergird co-making. Figuring out how to negotiate these tensions is where the implications of our study chiefly reside.

First, there is the relation to materials. Although the maker programs make every effort to procure the necessary materials and resources youth need for their projects—materials that change along with their iterative design features—sustaining funding and procuring a range of materials in-the-moment is challenging. Further, the youth are cognizant of designing innovations that fit the economic realities of the communities for whom they are designing. Youth have eschewed more expensive making materials (e.g., Peter and Kalvin rejected using littleBits snap-together electronics components for their baby gate project, due to cost) in favor of items accessible to their community.

Second, there is the tension around what we have referred to as sustained engagement within a context of complicated lives. Interrupted attendance was not unusual due to both living situations and home/school demands. These interruptions precipitate frustration for the youth as their making sometimes progresses in fits and starts, and maker educators are often required to engage in tailored "catch-up" activities with interrupted youth. Interrupted youth also often felt "behind" when they rejoined the maker club and witnessed the progress their more consistent peers had made. Yet such interruptions appear to be mediated by an approach to sustained making that expands the boundaries of making, but that frames the complexities of living as integral to the wisdom to make, to suggest what sustained making can encompass for youth living their lives in their context. When Samuel missed 2 months because of transient home conditions, he used that time to "think and think" about his project. Upon his return, he had a maker teacher who framed that thinking as essential to the critical work of making.

The adult maker educators across the two sites take a firm anti-deficit stance toward the youth's making and all have experience working with youth in educational settings. As the goal of both sites was to co-negotiate a community maker culture that empowers youth makers, explicitly engaging in community ethnography with the youth was a pedagogical commitment adult maker educators made. Their expertise in supporting youth in crafting surveys and interview questions was instrumental in facilitating the community ethnography process. However, educators had to negotiate their own insider-outsider (insider to community making club, outsider to communities) positioning when helping youth analyze and make sense of community data. While educators sought to always privilege youth voices and insights, they had to negotiate their own impetus to suggest "solutions" too quickly. Figuring how and when to foreground the adult–maker educator identity (having more expertise than youth in making-related issues) and when to foreground the community insider-outsider identity (having fewer insights than youth in community issues) was challenging and involved "on the job" training.

Lastly, as the youth drew from and expanded their relevant funds of knowledge threads directly related to their making, owning and reliving these threads throughout the making process also served to remind the youth of a positionality marginalized by systemic racism and classism and the degree to which they are entrenched in matrices of oppression. Adult maker educators also experience tensions alongside the youth, as they seek to understand the viewpoints of the youth and engage in uncomfortable conversations, as part of the emerging maker culture at the community clubs. However, negotiating these tensions is necessary for the youth and adult maker educators to cultivate an authentic, empowering community-based maker culture grounded in justice-oriented norms, practices, and goals.

LOOKING AHEAD

Equity-oriented making is never separate from individual and social histories that unfold across space and time. Who can make and who cannot, whose knowledge matters and whose does not, are all a part of making itself. Everyday decisions in makerspaces inscribe not only what counts as authentic "making," but also youth identities as makers, participants, collaborators, community members, young people *who legitimately belong in this makerspace*, signifiers that endure as historicizing elements shaping the emerging culture of the youth makerspace. We argue that youth making anchored in community engagement, as we sought to design for, is a productive way to both honor youth's histories while fostering their agency to determine how and where their emerging histories, while reified in in-the-moment experiences through community ethnography, can be sought for in more just ways.

Supporting youth in co-making in community, in expansive and sustained ways, situates knowledge production within local contexts in decolonizing ways, helping disrupt normative power dynamics among youth, adults, and context. Through the iterative process of engaging community as a part of making, youth drew from their local knowledge as oppressed *and* empowered insiders, and forced attention on typically silenced narratives around low-income communities such as inadequate resources for child care, homelessness, rape, and bullying—narratives usually alien to typical public makerspaces (Norris, 2014). The youth claimed empowering spaces for themselves by using the tools of community ethnography and the resources and practices in making to bring to the open, often through tension-filled negotiations, the particular injustices in which they and their communities suffer.

Through their community-centered making work, youth demanded the widening of boundaries around the makeup of a community making space, in dialectical relationships with the salient identities of community youth makers. The landscape, population, and practices of a community making space are reshaped as a result. Who youth makers are, what issues they care about, who other stakeholders could be with whom youth makers can collaborate, what resources are sanctioned, and what approaches to take toward making an artifact are all renegotiated in ways that foster equitably consequential making for the youth. We believe that equity in STEM-rich making is possible when cocreated in locally centered community making spaces where youth can be empowered to collaboratively frame problems and design solutions to authentically address real injustices in their everyday lives.

CHAPTER 6

Making for a More Just World

As noted in Chapter 2, we recognize making as a historicized practice that takes place across space and time. It is always rooted in the history and geographies of young people's lives and in the broader context of making and makerspaces in the United States and beyond. But what does this mean for youth growing up in lower-income communities of color? How does their rootedness as insiders in their communities—and their access to community knowledge, experience, and relationships—map onto and disrupt their places of making?

Like Rubel et al. (2017), and as outlined in Chapter 2, we take a justice-oriented approach to making sense of place, foregrounding place as always being made up of layers of narratives and meaning. How those layers of meaning are made visible, by whom and for what purposes, is always tied to issues of power and position. For example, we, and the youth we work with, are deeply aware that dominant narratives in American society frame the place of lower-income communities of color as deficient. As the stories in this text reveal, and also as discussed elsewhere (Green, 2015), asset-based lenses for making sense of place powerfully position youth in more agentic ways. As one of the youth stated in defense of her city:

> Great Lakes City isn't boring as long as you get out. People say Great Lakes City is boring, but I have been around the whole Great Lakes City area. I have been to the east, west, north, and south side of Great Lakes City. I was even born on the south side of Great Lakes City. I am just going to tell people don't just down Great Lakes City because you haven't been out enough. Don't try to ruin someone else's fun of coming to Great Lakes City, because you thought it was lame or you thought it wasn't fun or you thought it was a depression to you.

Across the stories of this text thus far, we hope we have shown how the youth, time and again, take up complex and time-consuming projects to address concerns that they believe are important to their communities. From designing light-up birthday cards for family members when store-bought cards are too expensive or too impersonal to prototyping sexual assault alarm jackets for teenage girls, the youth's making practices reflect a desire to engage the multiple and intersecting places of community while also challenging what it means to become in STEM.

In this chapter, we will consider the places of making: the making space itself, the communities in which youth participate across their lives, and STEM. We explore in more detail how youth make with, in, and for their communities in ways that both challenge and transform these places of making. As we do so, we seek to maintain the complexity of these places of making, in their multiple and layered ways, especially as brought to life by the youth as community ethnographers and makers (Taylor & Hall, 2013).

In building this argument we develop two main claims. First, youth's making practices are rooted in the knowledge, experiences, histories, and relationships of and in community. That is, making with and in community opened opportunities for youth to project the ordinariness of childhood and the rich culture of their communities onto their making, while also making visible the historicized injustices they experience in the world, and the symbolic and physical violence they sometimes experienced as a result. A critical aspect is in how youth sought to reclaim their experiences, lives, and communities in more complex and agentic ways than what dominant narratives imply. Such agentic acts are both carefully considered yet organic, and often risky. Second, we suggest that youth's making practices iteratively and incrementally built on one another in ways that *transformed the places of making*. In other words, the youth leveraged a kind of Mobilities of Criticality in their STEM-rich making toward empowered place-making. Such empowered place-making, as we discuss in this chapter, is important, for it facilitates or constrains opportunities to learn and become legitimate makers.

To develop these claims, and to show how they differentially play out in practice, we share two in-depth stories of youth makers: Jennifer and Emily and the heated jacket, and Samuel and the light-up football.

STORIES OF YOUTH MAKERS

Jennifer and Emily's Heated Jacket

Jennifer and Emily. Jennifer and Emily joined their making club in autumn of their 6th-grade year. Jennifer joined because she wanted to use the computers. She found science "boring," and often complained that she was not allowed to "build" things or "use technology" in school science. However, she felt that she was good at using the computer and the Internet. She was proud of her efforts to get behind the firewall set up at the club or to jailbreak her mother's phone. As she stated: "I am good at jailbreaking stuff. I am actually good at jailbreaking. Like going on an iPad or iPod or whatever, it's like an unlock. You can jailbreak it and get inside of it." However, Jennifer told us that no one recognized her interest or ability with technology. For example, when teachers asked questions about computer skills and the Internet during class, Jennifer said she was the first one to raise her hand, even though she was rarely called on to help.

Emily, however, joined the club because Jennifer did. The two had been best friends from an early age. They came to the local community club together after school because both of their mothers worked during the after-school hours, and their school did not provide after-school programs. Emily felt that the making club gave her something to do with her friend that was interesting.

In this vignette, we describe their design work in the 7th grade, where they eagerly returned to participate in their making club for a second year.

→ bk safety was a concern

The Heated Jacket. Over 8 months, from October to May, Jennifer and Emily designed a heated jacket. In the shoulders of the jacket they sewed in flexible solar panels. The panels were attached to rechargeable batteries, which would store the energy, and which would also power three small heating elements located within the layers of the jacket. They added a thin layer of Mylar insulation (a common resin polyester film used to make helium balloons, food packaging, and warming blankets) to the jacket to allow the smaller heating elements to adequately heat the jacket, and to cut down heat escape.

The girls came up with this idea after spending 4 weeks surveying peers and community members about the safety issues they cared about. They collected 62 survey responses. From graphs made of the data, the girls noticed that "commuting" was a main safety concern, identified by 74% of the respondents. When they looked closely at the comments written by the respondents, they noted that youth respondents were more concerned with walking in the dark and with bullying than the adult respondents.

They opted to design a heated and lighted hooded sweatshirt. The girls described their project as a sweatshirt that would be "warm and bright," and that would also be "lightweight and beautiful." Emily described the shirt this way: "There are a lot of people who get frostbite in the winter when people are outside. Ours is way cheaper than a regular sweatshirt and way warmer. It will keep you warm and snug. It will have a heater in it and lights for glamour and fashion." (See Figure 6.1.)

Samuel and the Light-Up Football

Samuel. Samuel joined his makerspace club when he was in the 6th grade. He had been "wanting to join for a while" but needed to wait until he was in 6th grade. Although he did not have friends already in the maker club, he said he wanted to join because he "kept seeing" what other kids were doing, and he, too, wanted to do "something like that." He wanted to be able to "do stuff with my hands, be active and stuff."

However, transportation issues caused Samuel to miss 2 months of club activities. This missed time was a setback for him. His first day back occurred on the first major "community feedback cycle" day in early January, when the youth in his club shared their work to date with local engineers and community members, who provided insights and ideas. His peers had already created three-dimensional printouts of their project ideas, had notebooks full of sketches and research, and had prepared short videos explaining their ideas. All Samuel had to share was his idea—a light-up football—an idea he had been "thinking and thinking and thinking" about at home. He wanted to make something that would "help kids make friends" and "keep them safe" when they played. We encouraged him to share his idea with the different visitors. One visiting science teacher pushed Samuel to put his ideas on paper. Together, they drew a model of what his light-up football might look like. In the process, Samuel and the visiting science teacher discussed the position of the lights: Where on the football should the lights be so that the entire ball can be seen in the dark? How could he ensure that the lights were not protruding on the football, so that the shape and smoothness of the football was not compromised?

Figure 6.1. Jennifer and Emily's Heated Jacket

The Light-Up Football. Samuel designed a prototype of a "light-up football" while working in an after-school community-based makerspace over 5 months. His football had LED tube lights that wrap around the ball to provide maximum lighting with minimal added weight, friction, or power expenditures. The efficient lighting was important because it would save on power, and keep "kids' hands from getting burnt." The lights were powered with rechargeable batteries that could be recharged at a solar docking station, limiting environmental impact and further saving money. Samuel constructed the actual football out of Nerf material in order to minimize added weight and to reduce the possibility of injury if one were to be hit in the head. The batteries were stored in a pocket at the center of the ball, accessible by a small door, to keep the football weighted properly and to keep the batteries from contact with rainwater and sweat. Samuel successfully completed his football, and a picture of him with his ball and a local football star hung proudly on the main wall of the community center's cafeteria.

The idea for a light-up football grew out of Samuel's desire to make something that would be helpful to people in his community. He knew that lighting was a concern at night due to limited working streetlights in his neighborhood. He also felt that the game of football was a positive peer activity that helped young people his age make friends and stay out of trouble. He knew that most families could not afford an expensive toy, and that inefficient designs were costly to the environment as well. He was proud of his efforts. As he stated, "I was really proud because it just made me feel good about myself so I could, like, kinda, acknowledge people what I could do. . . . Like make what I did, a light-up football. I wanna make more stuff like that." (See Figure 6.2.)

ROOTED IN COMMUNITY

Practices as Rooted in Community

Through their making, the youth identified and responded to problems that affected themselves but were also deeply linked to their community's unique history and context. They positioned both themselves and their making in place—as a part of their local ecology, rather than outside of it. Relph (1976) first proposed the insideness-outsideness dialectic to illustrate how one's sense of place exists as "a full range of possible awareness, from simple recognition for orientation, through the capacity to respond empathetically to the identities of different places, to a profound association with places as cornerstones of human existence and individual identity" (p. 63). In schools, teachers and students are rarely asked to identify with place. The very notion that one can position oneself as inside or outside of place stands in stark contrast to the driving norm in science

Figure 6.2. Samuel's Light-Up Football

education, where the focus is on generalized, "across the board" scientific knowledge and practice. However, in taking on local problems, in community spaces, youth used their insider knowledge and status to frame the problem space, and to work toward community-sustaining solutions (Rubel et al., 2017).

The youth imbued their making projects with wisdom and hope, in ways that drew upon their community insider funds of knowledge, experiences, and relationships. For example, knowledge of where streetlights have historically not worked, why kids at their school get bullied, fashion and the part it plays in school/neighborhood culture, how to work with one's hands to build, or the reasons and impacts of major economic concerns of the home, all reflect their insideness—their membership and experiences in the community places that they inhabit. How the youth drew from these funds across places reflected their attempts to seek connections in traversing between community places and their STEM-infused youth making clubs. These different points of intersection, as we describe later, became meaningful sites of negotiation.

Thus, the youth's making practices, as rooted in a wide range of community places, drew upon (and incorporated) *expert knowledge* on issues inherent to these places privy only to insiders, such as the funds of knowledge one has because of where they have grown up, and with whom (Moll, Neff, & Gonzalez, 1992). These practices also incorporated insider positioning *status*, such as that granting access to the social networks and contexts necessary for gaining deeper insights and access to resources when needed.

If we look at Samuel's light-up football, we can see how he was keen on making this football because he wanted to help keep his peers and the younger children in his community safe. He stated that his motivation for this project was his care for the people in his community: "[My football] say about me that I really care about people. And I could do stuff in the community, do stuff together, like peers can do stuff together, like neighbors or school neighbors could go outside and do stuff together. . . . 'Cause, like, some kids don't really play football, don't have no friends and stuff, so I go find people to help out a little bit."

Samuel's idea of care is nested in an understanding of the particular needs of the young people in his community. He lives in a neighborhood where there are limited streetlights (not uncommon in lower-income neighborhoods in the United States, where city infrastructure breaks down due to systemic underfunding), and where there is gang activity. He also lives in the far northern part of the country, where daylight hours are short for the majority of the school year, and when play is limited to the after-school hours. The lack of working streetlights makes it difficult to see the football and to see others, potentially making it unsafe to play. As he stated, "Well, when little kids are playing outside football and it's getting too dark, and they still keep playing and somebody might get hit in the head or something 'cause they can't see the ball really, so I'm going to light up the football so you can see where it's going."

Samuel was also worried about his peers who do not have friends. He viewed football as a way to bring young people together in safe ways. From Samuel's perspective, a light-up football would have wide appeal. He believed a light-up football could bring kids together who may find the lights cool, even if they do not like football. As Samuel stated, "I think other people will like my invention. Because, like, some kids like stuff that glows in the dark, so kids, like, some kids like my cousins, they play football, they're on the football team, so they'd probably like the football that glows outside and throw around and stuff to get better at the—for next year—for the next season they play football."

In addition to insider knowledge, insider status played a role in the youth's making practices. That is, having insider status enabled the youth to tap into informal social networks for the right kind of help in acquiring such funds, or how to do so. For example, Jennifer and Emily were not sure, initially, what to make. In gathering survey data to give them ideas for the problems their communities wanted solved, they were able to, with their peers, get 62 youth and adults to respond. They knew they could stand by the club's main entrance to get input from parents, and they knew which neighborhood stores would allow them to talk to patrons. They walked around the neighborhood pointing out which houses *more respected when gathering if an data insider* (handwritten margin note)

and apartments were good places to stop to ask for survey input. Here, their status as insiders helped them to be respected by others in the community toward gathering data.

Further, when they examined their data, they noticed that "commuting" was the main safety concern, identified by 74% of the respondents (n=46). However, in the open-ended comments, they noticed the concern raised about getting to places safely when it is cold and dark. In reflecting upon this pattern in their data, Jennifer raised a connection to her own experiences: She recalled a time when her mom took her horseback riding, a "very special trip" because it was not a typical family outing. However, the day was cold. Without access to warmer clothing, Jennifer had gotten "so cold," she could "not feel her hands," and they had to end horseback riding early, and she missed her opportunity to fully experience something she had "always dreamed of doing." She did not want other children to have that same experience. These two experiences served as the impetus for their idea: the lighted, heated jacket.

Practices as Enactments of Youth's Deep and Critical Knowledge and Wisdom Based on Their Insider Status

Many of the funds deployed by the youth in their making practices were grounded in nodes of criticality, located in place. By nodes of criticality we mean places of response to the injustices young people face growing up. All communities face risks that result from geographical, socioeconomic, and political challenges. However, the risks are greater for young people growing up in places where they are experiencing higher levels of environmental and social injustice. Many of the youth we worked with in this study live in multigenerational poverty. Unemployment in their communities remains high, and government spending on things such as infrastructure (e.g., streetlights) has been severely cut. The youth did not view these as barriers as much as they viewed them as conditions that required a response, because, in one young woman's words, "the government isn't doing its job."

Further, these young people valued their communities and the positive experiences they have there, from participating in programs at their club to a strong sense of community within their churches and neighborhoods. They also value their rich culture in faith, music, fashion, and community action. The youth were protective of their community. That they leveraged their more critical funds toward solving local problems is important.

This stance is significant, for it reflects an engagement with criticalities that is forward directed toward empowered social futures, even as it challenges deficit narratives in the moment.

We see such criticality enacted by these youth in their making work as tied to four domains in particular: *economic* (e.g., making their designs affordable); *environmental* (e.g., creating designs that reduce their communities' carbon footprint and support local ecologies); *social* (e.g., fostering positive peer relationships, healthy well-being, and community ownership, and preventing bullying and gang activity); and *urban infrastructure* (e.g., providing lighting and warmth on cold, dark days).

For example, Samuel worried about peer friendships and believed some of these peer-related challenges might be remedied with positive play, such as with a football. Samuel persisted in refining his football so that it met the needs of a wide range of peers. He first sought peer input on lighting—weight and design. He then pushed for input on weighting and feel. He tested his football with peers his age and peers younger than him. He pressed them for feedback on what functionality they needed, which is why he ultimately sought to make sure his ball was waterproof. Each interaction required Samuel to consider many new technical factors in his design that he had not previously considered (e.g., safety of material, not burning hands, waterproof), but he was deeply motivated by how and why his football would serve his local peer community.

Another design dimension important to Samuel related to his continued concern about safety. He was committed to make the football a safe toy—one that would not burn hands or contribute to a head injury.

First, in choosing his lighting, he opted to use LED lighting, even though it was more expensive in production, because it is more energy efficient, reduces energy costs and environmental impact, and because very little energy is converted to heat, so the LED lights would not burn the players' hands. Given that his target audience involved "6-year-olds and up," keeping hands safe was important. As he stated, "Yeah, I learned about the LED lights, they, uh, they're not hot—hot—hot, like, like the regular batteries, I mean, not the light. They don't get so hot, so 'cause they're real bright but it's like they save energy so it won't be like, if you throw it or touch the light it won't, like, burn your hand."

Second, in choosing football material, he opted to use a soft, foam, Nerf-style ball. In talking with his mom, whom he did not see often, he became convinced this would help kids be safer if they got hit in the head: "Yeah, I asked my mom and she said that, if you mean, like, [. . .] this football, like, so if somebody tries to catch it and they get hit in the head it won't be so hard. So I used, like, a foam one, so it could be, like, when you catch it or get hit, your head, will be, like, soft. So it won't, like really hurt that much." This seems particularly salient because much of the "off-season" practices happen informally without access to helmets or pads.

Likewise, Jennifer and Emily noted the twin challenges of keeping warm in the winter and of getting bullied for one's clothing choices, especially when clothing options are limited due to family finances. They described their project as a sweatshirt that would be "warm and bright," and that would also be "lightweight and beautiful." The girls wanted the jacket to be lightweight so that they were not restricted to a lumpy, thick jacket—very unfashionable—to keep warm. Costly winter jackets typically tout slimness as a key, attractive feature. Jennifer's design would, as she stated, be "beautiful but with casual in it so that you don't expose yourself." People would not be able to make fun of you for clothes that had "stains" or were "ugly."

The aesthetics of the shirt carried deeper meaning than just beauty, in light of these criticalities. Both girls loved fashion, and both were concerned about inappropriate exposure and also about being bullied for their appearance. As someone who had been bullied herself for appearance, this was an important concern for Jennifer: "I was, like, I am going to give you something beautiful but with casual in it so that you don't expose yourself. Like a jacket that goes all of the way down." "My idea could help change things. People make fun of you . . . 'Why are you wearing that? You are ugly. There are stains on your clothes.'" The potential for being bullied was important, as both girls described having been bullied for their appearance—for example, being told, "You are ugly" or "Hey, nappy-head."

Pivot Points and Their Functions

As youth engaged in community-rooted making practices over time, their in-the-moment actions served as "pivot points" in their design work. Here we refer to Holland and Lave's (2001) use of the term *pivot* to refer to "mediating or symbolic devices" not just to "organize responses but also to pivot or shift into the frame of a different world" (Holland & Lave, 2001, p. 50). When youth leveraged their community funds of knowledge and wisdom, for example, toward work on their projects, they etched their insideness onto their engineering design, in ways that impacted the design process and how/where it unfolds, as well as their role in it. As pivots, these funds were not simply complementary to the youth's engineering design, but *essential* to *both who they are and their design work*.

Pivot points included *tools* (e.g., sewing machine, Google SketchUp), *relationships* (e.g., Samuel's ties to his cousins and peers) and the *innovations* themselves (e.g., Samuel's light-up football), all of which were able to shift the nature of STEM engagement for the youth, and potentially transform their possibilities for becoming and being within particular places (e.g., Samuel's peers and cousins engaging in safe play at night in their neighborhood).

We illustrate the importance of pivots in Figure 6.3. Here, we see how pivots mediate youth's rootedness in community toward empowered making. These pivots facilitated movement between different framings—including STEM inquiry, making, community, and action taking—that pushed youth's making, in how they provided (a) navigational indicators for launching project work or delving more deeply into

Figure 6.3. Pivots and Their Functions

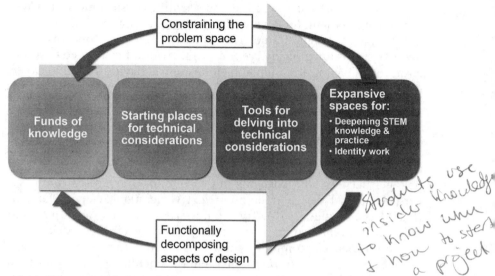

technically-oriented design work, and (b) social negotiation toward legitimizing multiple perspectives and points of entry into making.

Navigational indicators. The youth often used their funds of knowledge as navigational indicators to launch new projects or to take new directions in current projects. We have been concerned with how youth locate productive starting places for projects. Such initial location work can be challenging, for it involves social negotiations of whom to work with, along with considerations of what challenges might be worth spending time on. In both cases presented in this manuscript, as well as in many of the cases from the larger study, the youth leveraged their funds as navigational indicators to author a productive project launching place. As Samuel noted in his interview, his light-up football was an idea he thought a long time about while he was home and unable to find transportation to the club. His experiences with limited streetlights, personal safety, and friendships became points of negotiation for how and with whom he would work.

In their club, the youth were charged with a fairly wide-open making task: Design something that "uses portable energy" and solves a problem or fills a need.

First, their insideness provided *secure direction* when the way forward in STEM was unclear. It also gave them direction for where, within their social network, they might look for help. For example, most of the youth shared initial design ideas that were attentive to *specific* community concerns, but initially framed through fairly *vague* technical and scientific terms. However, they leveraged their specific insider knowledge of community concerns as pivots to delve into the technical dimensions of their work. This kind of pivot point was particularly important in helping the youth grapple with technical and scientific considerations that were challenging to them; they were able to pivot and shift into the "technical dimensions of design" frame. The specific community concerns helped the two groups functionally break down the work they needed to accomplish from a technical standpoint—for example, having a need to experiment with power requirements and conducting challenging calculations. This is important given the new focus in the science education standards in the United States on supporting students in systematically refining design constraints and in evaluating possible solutions toward optimization, through multiple cycles of prototyping solutions, designing/conducting tests toward optimizing solutions, gathering/analyzing data from multiple perspectives, and engaging in dialogue on complicated conflicts in perspective and design trade-offs (Next Generation Science Standards [NGSS] Lead States, 2013). Their funds also gave them pivot points for where, within their social network, they might look for feedback.

Second, specific community concerns raised in the moment provided a *safe space* for youth to *critique* their efforts, opening up spaces for them to functionally break down design work into reasonable bits from a technical standpoint. As community concerns initiated more complex design conditions, the youth had to turn to the science to consider the best ways to both maximize trade-offs and optimize their designs. As one youth stated, "We need to feel safe when we are learning these things."

For example, community input raised new complex challenges for Samuel over the months he worked on his project. He needed to consider how to power his lights, as well as how to make his football brighter, lighter, and more stable. As a result, Samuel needed to deepen his knowledge of energy systems and environmental and economic impact. Working with a mentor, Samuel figured out how to calculate power requirements of different lighting systems. This technical task was one that became salient once his peers pointed out that his chosen lighting system required too many batteries. He also read information on the Internet on the affordances of LED lights, when his friends told him that bulky lights would not work on the football. He spent time figuring out how to assemble the components in a circuit with a switch so that the batteries would not be wasted in daylight.

Let us look at Samuel's project development in more detail for a moment. Recall that Samuel's rootedness in community positioned him with expert knowledge and status on football and the dimensions of safety surrounding football play in the dark as well as what it meant to grow up in a low-income urban community.

Samuel's launching point into design was his desire to figure out how to power his ball in an affordable way. In fact, powering the lights was, in

Samuel's words, his "biggest design challenge." He had gotten an old football from home, and he had found strip LEDs in his making club. His initial idea was to use rechargeable batteries to power the light strips "so we can see all the time but so you won't have to keep going back to the store and buying, like, batteries to reuse." Saving both money and time by not having to return to the store to buy new batteries were both important in order for Samuel to keep the lights powered. Rechargeable batteries, however, also addressed another design concern: Samuel's care for the environment. He was worried about the problems created when non-rechargeable batteries are thrown into the trash. As he stated, "When you throw batteries away, and those critters can get inside your trash, like the raccoons can take your batteries, take your trash and batteries out. So to leave the batteries everywhere, so they can eat it and stuff. I didn't want that to happen, so I made it so it could be rechargeable batteries. The batteries can just be used on and on again."

After deciding upon rechargeable batteries, he noted in his sketch-up notebook that he needed to find a way to make his ball bright enough without using too many batteries in order to keep the cost and weight down. Samuel wrote that two batteries did not light the ball well enough to see for "100 yards," but more than two batteries made the football too heavy and expensive.

Drawing upon relationships (one form of pivot) Samuel sought input on these concerns from his friends. He noted that his friends were concerned that the ball was too heavy and bulky from the lights. They wanted the ball to be lighter so that it could go farther. They suggested that he remove some of the lights so that they would not "make it heavier" and "pull it to the ground."

Samuel then decided to spend time searching for information on the Internet (another form of pivots, tools) on the affordances of LED lights, when his friends told him that bulky lights would not work on the football. He sought out "different LED lights" as not all LED are "the same." He opted for LED tube lighting "because it's a tube and you can, like, stretch it around the whole football. So, what I did was, I had it made so when you throw it, it could get more spin and then you could see the light very well." This seemed to solve several of his problems.

Samuel also initially worked with a mentor, to figure out how to calculate power requirements of different lighting systems and how to put a switch into his system so that the batteries would not be wasted in daylight. These more challenging technical tasks became salient once his peers pointed out his chosen lighting system required too many batteries.

Samuel then drew further upon his community relationships (form of pivots) with local football experts, which included a local football player, who starred at the local university and who is active at his community center, and his cousins, who play for local community teams. When recounting how these different experts helped him in his design, Samuel noted that the football star helped him think about how to make the ball balanced, so that it would not be too heavy on one side or the other. To solve this problem, Samuel had to cut deeply into his prototype to place the batteries in the far center:

> I changed a lot, like, make sure it's not so heavy, so like, if you throw it, it's not going to go far as a regular football. So when I met with "TD," we was outside throwing the football around and he said that, my football is, that, it's like a regular NFL quarterback player throws it, it'll go just like a regular football. . . . So I used that, and so when I went back and tried to do it, I made sure that when I cut it, I made sure that it could be deep enough so it won't, like, make it so heavy. So it could be, not be so light [referring to weight distribution], it could be just right. So *like a real NFL football.*

Samuel asked the football star to comment further on the feel of the football. He wanted to know if the football felt "comfortable when you throw it" and "how far can you throw it, if it's heavy or light?" Video footage shows Samuel passing the football to the star so that he could throw it. TD, the local football star, then said, "How far can you throw it? Well, this is probably about as heavy as a real football, so you could probably, depending on who the quarterback is or whoever is throwing it, you could probably throw it the same distance as a real football."

In this example, we see how the initial launching point of wanting to power the ball in an economically and environmentally efficient way led Samuel to further consider more complex technical challenges, including type and location of lighting and weighting and location of weight. Relationships, tools, and innovations served as critical pivots in helping Samuel navigate the making process in ways that drew upon his rootedness in community and insider knowledge, and provided places for delving more deeply into STEM. We illustrated this pathway in the processes of leveraging Mobilities of Criticality in Table 2.1.

We see a similar process of iterative making unfolding in Emily and Jennifer's jacket, especially when they became stuck and frustrated. In one instance, Emily and Jennifer found that moving from their ideas and sketches of jackets to actual hands-on design work was difficult. During the initial phase of the project, they delved into the project by spending several hours on Pinterest and Google, looking for ideas on hoodie designs and approaches to lighting and heating. This online exploration led to many different ideas for the hoodie, including clearer ideas of what they did *not* want to do. "All of the heated jackets are for hunting and construction, not for casual." "Look, they all have those big heating parts, and that would be heavy!" "That would waste too much electricity." "That is just too much and too much money."

In another instance, after one of the mentors had given the girls suggestions on how they might test the power requirements of the different heating pads they selected for possible use in their project, the girls pushed that activity aside for their own tests focused on comfort and looks. The activity involved measuring the amps and volts the heater needed and calculating the total power requirements for their design for a specified usage period. Then they had to measure and calculate the amps and volts each rechargeable AA battery could send. By comparing the two figures, they could then determine how many batteries their design might need.

They designed tests for measuring how soft the heating pad was, how warm the jacket got and how comfortable that warmth was, and whether the heating element fit well inside the jacket they planned to modify. These tests led the girls to select the largest heating pad, because it scored the highest on each of these concerns. One of the mentors stepped in at this point, and asked the girls how many rechargeable batteries it would take to power their system. When they did not know, she worked with them on the power requirement calculations they had shunned earlier. Together, they spent nearly 90 minutes on this task. They figured out that if they wanted to power the heating pad, they would need 101 AA batteries to do so. Emily threw her arms up in despair and said they couldn't do it; they didn't have enough batteries even if they wanted to.

Their mentor reminded the girls of a video diary they had made earlier on insulation, and she suggested that they go back and watch it to get some ideas. The girls watched and laughed at their video, seemingly breaking down the tensions that surfaced at the frustrations of their calculations. However, the video involved a reflection on Jennifer's experiences at home with their fireplace and the insulation her father had put around it. The fireplace became central the previous winter when their home was without electricity for 2 weeks because of a powerful winter storm. She explained, "When we had that big snowstorm here and everyone's power went out. The silver lining, I seen a lot of it, because we had to put it in our fire place. We had to put silver lining around it so the heat would stay in it, but it wouldn't burn anything outside of it." Jennifer and Emily asked us if we could get them some "silver lining" material to help them "keep the heat in" and if we had any ideas for smaller heating elements that would "only take two batteries."

Like Samuel, the girls drew upon pivots in crucial moments to advance their making in ways that foregrounded their rootedness. The pivots, including both tools (such as Internet searches, Pinterest, experimenting with AA batteries and heating pads) and relationships (with adult mentors and family members), also granted directionality to the "next steps" the youth took in the making process. However, the girls seemed to encounter more visible stuck moments, which nearly stopped forward progress, with more intensity than did Samuel. Each time, the youth returned to their rootedness or to critical pivots, enabling them to figure out how to relaunch their project.

Social Negotiation. As the youth leveraged different pivots in novel ways, they created moments of social negotiation toward *legitimizing* multiple perspectives and entry points in STEM-rich making. For example, Samuel drew upon ideas from many different people he had relationships with in his life, as he sought ideas for his design and positioned himself as an interested learner and designer, caregiver, football expert, and friend. His mom provided insight on safety related to head injuries, and this prompted Samuel to use a softer foam material. His peers provided feedback on weight, size, lighting, and use in the rain. The football star tested the ball for comfort, distance, and feel. At the same time, Samuel sought help from technical experts, such as energy engineers, to consider issues of energy transformations involved in lighting, helping him select energy-efficient lights that would not burn hands. These experts also provided insight into how he might cut the football so that he could get the batteries inside the ball rather than having them hang on the outside, as he had originally positioned them. All of these people and resources mattered in helping him bring his design to fruition.

Through the use of pivots, youth further established connections between the different places where they are insiders (e.g., maker club itself versus community club that houses maker club), both broadening and thickening the networks that can serve STEM mobilities. These expanding social networks helped to elevate the youth's funds of knowledge as important in scientific and technical investigation. This was accomplished through new forms of practice that remade the places of their work.

For example, when Jennifer cut too far into the jacket, both she and Emily thought she had ruined it. They did not have another jacket to use, and both were ready to give up. In the next session, one of the mentors brought a sewing machine to the maker club so that Jennifer and Emily could fix their jacket. When Jennifer saw the sewing machine, she asked if she could bring one of community center's staff members to the maker room. She said, "I know Ms. Y. can use the sewing machine. She told me before. I remember it!" Ms. Y. showed Jennifer how to use the sewing machine and helped her sew with it. Jennifer kept her eyes on Ms. Y. and tried to learn everything that Ms. Y. showed her. Several young people took an interest in what Jennifer was doing with the sewing machine. After Ms. Y. left the maker room, Jennifer taught her new sewing skills to the others in the room, positioning herself with important and shareable expertise. Learning to use this tool helped her identify with the process of iterative design. As she says, "This is me making a horrible mistake by cutting it, and so I had to learn how to sew. But next time if something breaks, I know how to sew it back together."

Although youth's making practices were shaped by the structures of the places where they worked—normative practices around engineering design, the tools and resources made available in their makerspace, the technical knowledge brought in by their mentors—their enactments of their deep and critical knowledge of and care for community also influenced activity within these places. Such performances reshaped these places in the moment, but also provided new pathways for future makers to traverse. The youth were creating and claiming new territories in place-making. As Jennifer and Emily spent time on Pinterest, showing others their ideas and creating pages of pinned designs, they also created new places for Jennifer's technology interests to flourish in her work, to position themselves as fashion experts among their peers, and to share ideas with others on what to do when you are stuck (e.g., use Pinterest). This is similar to Cresswell's (2014) analogy of place-making in a public park, where people ignore the bisecting pathways in favor of a diagonal shortcut through the grass. Such performances give way to new mud paths through the park for current and future park goers.

MAKING FOR PLACE AND PLACE-MAKING

The youth's making practices iteratively and incrementally built on one another to expand the students' STEM expertise and rootedness in community. Both the merging and layering of STEM and their funds of knowledge onto *and* into each other were accomplished not only in the design work, but also *in the attempt to change the places in which the youth are working and becoming.* In other words, the youth leveraged a kind of Mobilities of Criticality in their making toward empowered place-making. Such empowered place-making, as we discuss below, is important, for it facilitates or constrains opportunities to learn and become legitimate makers. That some of the youth have said they want to get smarter on these topics so that they can return to their community—not leave it as they move on up—speaks to this point well. In short, new possibilities in place-making operate at the level of the making process *and* at the level of the potential impact of the youth-created innovation.

In particular, we believe that insights gleaned from youth's Mobilities of Criticality help show how learning as movement calls attention to how movement can importantly involve critical engagement with "the word and the world" (Freire, 1970). This stance foregrounds the agency that the youth have through their making to push toward new formations of place, with material and social configurations that allow for new patterns of participation. Such new formations of place expand upon who and what is recognized within dynamic networks of practice in order to disrupt participation boundaries and knowledge hierarchies.

In many ways, what we see across our data is a kind of place-making that deterritorializes STEM routines and practices, making "physical entry into and living in previously forbidden places" a process of taking back and reclaiming the place of STEM in ways that recognize and care for the rootedness of young people (Perumal, 2015, p. 26). We see, in particular, youth's Mobilities of Criticality highlighting the intersecting forms of place-making that require attention in the field: making spaces, community, and STEM/discipline.

Place-Making Occurs Incrementally

In terms of the "place" of *making spaces* (one area of place-making), we see a gradual and incremental emergence of a youth-centered making culture. As youth iteratively refined the problem and optimized their designs in both technical and social ways, they expanded their connectedness to others, and their access to ideas, tools, and resources for advancing their developing expertise. Here, we see such incremental transformation of place occurring as youth perform place as they use it (Lombard, 2014) toward becoming in ways that make possible their hoped-for social futures. As Samuel walked through the main club rooms with his ball, kids gathered around him asking to test it out, and where and when they could buy one. His picture with the pro football star hangs on the wall, and other youth have since joined the club to "do what Samuel did," which included "making" things and "meeting famous people." As youth adorned the walls with their efforts, both in progress and final, these artifacts materially and socially changed the space to support forms of making that mattered to the youth there. Here, the youth often resisted the construction of expectations about making practices through normative making by using their making place in subversive ways (Cresswell, 2014).

Intersecting Scales of Place-Making: Impacting Both Making Club and Communities

Further, the youth's making occurred both in the making space room itself, and outside of it, making the boundaries more porous. Becoming an expert involved vertical development in deepening scientific knowledge and practice. Expertise also took new forms as youth moved ideas and practices horizontally, weaving in experiences, knowledge, and practice from other domains such as football, friendships, bullying, and caring for others. For Samuel, the making space expanded beyond the walls of the making area into peer activities on the football field. It transformed in the new social networks of people he brought into his expanded makerspace. Emily and Jennifer generatively transformed the making space with each new activity they took up, often in resistance to the more traditional making activities. Including fashion and bullying as a part of the discourse of making transformed who, and what, were legitimized resources for the place. We see this in the criteria they applied to the selection of solar panels (e.g., flexible solar panels that could be made glamorous).

The youth's designs helped transform the place of *in community* (another area of place-making) for themselves and their peers. Jennifer and Emily's jacket makes warmth and fashion affordable. Samuel's football will allow his peers to practice throughout the off-season, so that they can "get better at the—for next year—for the next season they play football."

Each new iteration of design, from refining the problem space to designing a working prototype, offered new and different opportunities for these practices to build toward future identity work, relationships, and recognized ways of being and doing in these different and interconnecting places. When Jennifer and Emily became stuck on some of the technical challenges of heating the jacket, they stepped back to take on a different technical challenge suggested by their peers: to make a 3-D logo for their jacket in Google SketchUp, as their friends insisted it was important for everyone to know that their jacket was made by them. Though this new task boundary was not essential to the functionality of the light-up or heat-up features of the jacket, it was necessary for both fashion and ownership. Like the FUBU (For Us By Us) hip-hop clothing line, these clothes were designed within the community for the community, and this was significant to potential wearers.

Place-Making in STEM

Equally as significant are the broad heterogeneous *places of STEM*, both real and imagined (a third area of place-making). The youth's practices served as new tools to expand the very purposes and goals of engaging in science. Learning science has a purpose broader than "doing school" or even, in the progressive sense taken up in the Next Generation Science Standards, learning how to explain how the world works so that one can be engaged in informed citizenry. At the heart of each youth's design is an effort to work at the intersection of science and the public good, as a way to transform both (through the production of new structures that support and legitimize their practice, such as the very artifacts they create). Their engagement with the problem was not simply motivated by individual interest. Engagement was framed, in part, through collectively formed interests as they sought out feedback from a wide range of others, at the powered boundaries of race, power, care, and danger. These tensions demanded greater engagement with STEM, as they demanded more complex problems be considered. At the same time, these tensions made possible recognition within STEM worlds, while also exposing the challenges youth face in seeking recognition in these same worlds. The light-up football served as a pathway into non-gang friendships as well as a potential stepping-stone for acceptance into engineering at the local community college and university.

As Jennifer and Emily sought feedback on their Google SketchUp logos for their jacket, Jennifer was able to show off her tech expertise, something she was very proud of. As she sought feedback on the logos, others (mentors and peers) positively responded to the logos, recognizing this expertise. But, because the logo was also for a fashionable, light-up heated jacket, she had further opportunities to remind people of this other important work she was engaged in. When we asked Jennifer about this, she noted that if you ask others what she is known for they "will probably say fashion." When she brought earlier design work home, she reports that her sister exclaimed loudly, "Oh my God! *You* did this??!!"

This kind of repositioning in STEM amid these tensions is important as it illustrates how the youth leveraged Mobilities of Criticality to simultaneously attend to multiple scales of activity through their making project. We have found imprints of youth's rootedness in community in how they worked across scales of activity in their systematic efforts to refine their design constraints and evaluate possible solutions toward optimization. Samuel's positioning within different communities (maker peers, cousins, engineering and football experts), supported engagement in different scales of activity, expanding what he made and how he made it. He wanted to be sure his product worked well for his friends (focus on the local, relational scale), was affordable and safe (focus and critique at the economic and infrastructural scale), and was kind to the local biodiversity (focus and care at the local environmental scale).

However, attending to different scales of activity can be a contested process. Dominant discourses of place (cf., Friedmann, 2007) often position the youth as outsiders and nonexperts in science and engineering. As a young Black male growing up in a low-income household, Samuel is supposed to like football, but he is not expected to like or work hard in STEM. He is not expected to care for the environment, even though lower-income communities of color continue to face some of the greatest environmental injustices (Schlosberg, 2013). Though his peers readily took up the football as an attractive piece of sports equipment, Samuel was unable to bring his football to school, ultimately continuing to restrict the value of community insiderness in school settings. That his *physical education* teacher but not his *science* teacher was interested in the football suggests the profound difficulty that Samuel continued to face as he sought more formal recognition for his work in school settings. While we do see recognition of Samuel's expertise expanding across his growing social network, he still faced challenges. The local football star found his football acceptable, but his peers pushed for more revisions. This reality

low expectations are put on young people's engineering efforts + skills

suggests how deeply entrenched low expectations for young people's engineering efforts might be, even by allies. He worked hard on his project for more than 100 hours after school, delving into more complex design concerns. This example also shows how complicated the places of STEM can be for youth: Samuel had to negotiate becoming an expert among his peers, but then had to seek recognition from a wide range of others in doing so—from science teacher to physical education teacher to football star—and with varying degrees of success.

Jennifer and Emily's efforts toward place-making across scales also cast light on more distant places not easily transformed by their efforts. Jennifer told us, "[I recognized that on TV] girls can't do science and engineering. . . . It's another TV show. On one episode, all these boys, they let one girl in science club cause she was girly, and they said girls wouldn't [do] good at science. They were teasing the girl." Jennifer is neither girly nor the prototypical "tomboy." Her place at the science table as set up by media is much less clear, and not so easily influenced by her making work.

Still, Jennifer and Emily's jacket increased their opportunities to "do stuff"—explore, create, and innovate with STEM—and to be recognized by their peers, their mentors, parents, community members, and science and engineering experts for their work, at least impacting efforts at the more local scale (see also Vossoughi, Escudé, Kong, & Hooper, 2013).

We believe these three forms of place-making indicate the importance of paying attention to intersecting scales of activity in youth's efforts to make and place-make (Jurow & Shea, 2015). Understanding what matters to young people in their making requires us to make sense of how their lives are shaped by and shape social and institutional practices, and within that, the possibilities for imagining new forms of learning that extend traditional forms of expertise. This view calls into question traditional patterns of participation in learning in order to support youth (and their teachers) in expanding upon who and what areas of expertise are recognized and valued in order to disrupt participation boundaries and knowledge hierarchies. Local and sociohistorical contexts act as interconnected, dynamic sites of learning (Gutiérrez, 2012), where students and teachers, individually and collectively, can struggle to negotiate relationships between personal and sociohistorical narratives regarding what normative participation looks like and for whom (Holland & Lave, 2009).

LOOKING AHEAD

The youth's making practices, as rooted in community, allow for remaking the places of STEM, making, and community, in how the movement of people, ideas, and relationships interrupt practices and ways of being. The heated jacket is evidence that the two girls possess robust scientific and engineering expertise, a direct countering of their marginal science student status. That their hope was to "change things" about beauty and fashion so that people would not be bullied also speaks to engagement with other issues of criticality in their young lives as youth from low socioeconomic backgrounds. The beneficiaries of the design would be people like themselves who cannot afford trendy clothes and who are bullied because of it.

The youth remind us that we need to pay attention to the ways in which how they are rooted in community matters to how they engage with STEM-rich making. The youth further remind us how learning takes shape across places and time, in ways that challenge expectations for what it means to know, do, and have expertise in making. The youth's practices not only altered their own possibilities for becoming in STEM, but also opened up new possibilities for others. At the same time, their stories reveal that such a project is deeply political, for how youth's mobilities expand is tied to institutional, sociohistorical, and in-the-moment power dynamics.

While the youth are in constant critical dialogue with the different places they inhabit (and as they move ideas and resources across these places toward making a difference), this critical dialogue involves a negotiation of what they hope to accomplish and what is realistic. It involves a deep understanding of and care for their community, and a desire for their community to be transformed. It involves a way of seeing themselves as people who occupy multiple places simultaneously, while never losing sight of their home place as they hope for something better.

The criticality that youth brought to their STEM-rich making—and place-making—is not unique to them. We see similar engagement with the layers of place in youth's engagement in mathematics and place (Rubel et al., 2017), and in community mapping (Taylor, 2017). As Taylor (2017) writes of the youth in her study engaged in community mapping of locative literacy practices:

> In these final phases of sharing, young people synthetically layered their biographical experiences and their desires for the future on top of a map of the community to create a personal cartography. . . . As a participatory literacy, learning locative digital literacies along lines also supported youth in disrupting a process of community planning that has historically positioned youth as victims of, or victimizing, community health. (p. 568)

The youth's work, alongside these studies, suggest that leveraging both community insideness and scientific expertise is about much more than bridging these worlds. Although such bridging is important, what's essential is how this bridging makes possible new and more expansive opportunities to learn and to become in STEM. Indeed, in many ways youth's criticality speaks back against the accounts that frame their communities in deficit ways. At the same time, their enactment of their criticality through their making practices calls attention to the prosaic and micro-level processes involved in making spaces—STEM, maker, and community—more habitable.

CHAPTER 7

Seeding an Authentic Community Making Culture

> I want to make things that will help people, and encourage others to do better things for our community. I want to help others so that they can teach others, too, and make the world a better place. —Jasmine, 12 years old

In this chapter, we return to the idea raised in Chapter 1 about how makerspaces have been positioned as a significant grassroots movement supporting informal learning (Schrock, 2014). This literature documents how the movement grew from the ground up, "with hackers meeting in garages, crafting clubs in homes, or public spaces" (Peppler, 2017, p. 453), and with innovations spreading one at a time (Peppler & Bender, 2013). The term *grassroots* has significance because it calls attention to the ways in which the movement has been driven by the "end user" and not the "established power hierarchy" (Lee, King, & Cain, 2015, p. 2). The grassroots nature of the maker movement has focused, in particular, on moving people from consumers to makers of ideas and technologies.

The grassroots proliferation of making spaces has contributed to breaking down important power hierarchies within the technological realm. With makerspaces becoming more available, technical innovations are being reconfigured and relocated outside the technological corporate infrastructure (Birtchnell & Urry, 2012). With access to makerspaces, people are able, more than ever before, to develop and personalize innovative capabilities and production activities whereever they are, whenever they want, while hooking into widely dispersed social networks virtually and face-to-face. Furthermore, innovation can take a uniquely personal feel, addressing idiosyncratic needs and desires not well met by corporate mass production, redistributing knowledge within the hands of the end user. Yet, as Lee, King, and Cain (2015) point out, the grassroots metaphor for the spread, growth, and formalization of the maker movement has critical limitations, for it "does little to say how the 'grass' has been placed, whether it was started as seed or sod, why it took hold, how it spread, and what it needed in order to grow" (p. 2).

In Chapters 4 through 6, we looked closely at the projects and practices of youth makers, and considered how youth worked within the dialectics of community/STEM and expert/activist toward powerful making. Not only were youth making practices rooted in their community knowledge and wisdom, but also they challenged expectations for what it means to know, do, and have expertise in STEM-rich making. In this chapter, we consider the ways in which youth *spread* access and opportunity in making within their community—and as mediated by the youth's culture and sociohistorical context (Bang et al., 2013). In particular, we explore what we refer to as "community youth maker practices" that youth cocreated as they sought to spread and grow the reach of their making efforts into their community, and to equip their community with STEM-rich maker practices that draw strength from community knowledge and practice.

To do so, we examine two critical events—an electric art workshop and a stop-motion animation workshop—both activities prepared by youth over months and offered to members of their local communities. These two workshops were designed and enacted by youth toward sharing their developing STEM-rich making expertise through teaching other youth at their community clubs. These two events reflect fairly prototypical maker activities, commonly used with youth makers across a wide range of making contexts. Electric art involves using copper tape, LED lights, and a power source (typically small coin cell batteries) to make greeting cards and small trinkets. By engaging in electric art, participants learn about different kinds of circuits, and can leverage them toward their own particular creative desires. Stop-motion animation involves digital manipulation of objects and images in a time-lapse sequence. Youth learn about lighting and angles along with the productions of models, building props, characters, and storylines. Youth also learned about green screen technology, which they utilized in some of their stop-motion films.

What we are interested in is how and why youth sought to engage others in workshops on these topics, and what messages they sought to communicate to others about what it meant to make, who makes, and the purposes and reach of STEM-rich making. In particular, we are concerned with how youth purposefully sought to "re-make" electric art and stop-motion animation making—and the making culture—in support of such efforts with community. Here we use the term *re-make* to consider how the youth's agentic efforts to teach others STEM-rich making practices involved a process of both disrupting and recreating the narratives of making and maker knowledge/practices in sometimes subversive ways.

ORGANIZING FOR MATERIAL REIMAGININGS
AND NEW SOCIAL FUTURES

Electric Art and Green Energy Workshop

On a chilly October evening in Great Lakes City, 16 youth welcomed more than 100 visitors to the first-ever Electric Art & Green Energy Maker Workshop ("electric art workshop") at their community-based making space. Everyone at the club was invited to participate in the event, from children as young as 6 years old to parents. One of the main goals of the electric art workshop was, in Fall's words (see Chapter 2), to help other youth feel accomplished because of "what you learned, how you worked on it, and how others saw it and what it meant to them."

Filling up their own makerspace and an adjacent room, the youth transformed these spaces into lively celebration and learning environments where youth of all ages, as well as parents, could enter into the space to create their own electric art.

The youth decorated the rooms with projects and designs they made involving electrical circuits—from light-up canvases to alarm jackets. They also set up a series of making tables, where they located their many different planned stations meant to support their peers in finding their own inroads into electric art. There was a wide range of stations where young people could make light-up artifacts powered by traditional and renewable energy sources, such as light-up bracelets or wristbands, light-up mini bulletin boards, canvas art, and card designs (see Table 7.1). There were also activities meant to teach the children about energy, circuitry, and making, including activities involving multi-meters, soldering, renewable energy (e.g., hand cranks and solar panels), and power tools (see Figure 7.1).

In addition, the youth planned for "snack zones" and "chill zones," so that participating youth could enjoy electric art games designed by the youth, music, and food, especially if their maker projects became "frustrating" or they themselves, as the youth leaders, "needed to blow off steam." They also made available their bicycle, hacked to power smartphones by pedaling, to allow others to power their phones. To help visitors navigate the activities, they created a schematic, showing where different activities took place.

The youth planned the workshop over the course of 4 weeks, across 12 sessions (3 afternoons per week). Though some of the youth had some electric art and circuitry expertise, others were new and needed to develop their knowledge and practices. In preparing for the event, the youth made their own electric art, learning how to build different kinds of circuits and how to power them with different renewable sources of energy. They invented different kinds of switches for their circuits that drew upon the materials they had available and their own creativity. They

Figure 7.1. Electric Art Workshop

brainstormed different kinds of light-up fabrications that might be of in-*brainstorm* terest to young people, from light-up picture frames made out of popsicle *& discussed* sticks to crafty trinkets to jewelry, and prototyped these different ideas. *activities* They solicited input on these ideas from their friends. They used this pro- totyping process to figure out what activities would be most interesting to their peers, what approaches would lead to durable and usable products, and what technical knowledge, skills, and challenges they needed to fig- ure out to help others. They also helped one another learn how to solder, use multi-meters, and troubleshoot problem circuits.

The week before the event, they formed small teams to further plan and refine making stations on the ideas they came up with, putting care- ful attention into how they would decorate the room and organize youth movement throughout the room.

Stop-Motion Animation Workshop

In December, just before the winter recess, youth at a community maker club in Gladtown hosted a "Big Brother Big Sister Stop Motion Movie Workshop" (stop motion movie workshop) for their younger peers (ages

Table 7.1. Electric Art Stations

Station	Youth Leaders	Activities	STEM-Making Focus
Electric Greeting Cards		Creating cards for friends and loved ones using copper tape, LED lights, batteries, and crafts	• How to build simple circuits • How to creatively design switches with crafts
Light-up Bracelets and Wristbands	Ginger, Kyneika	Creating decorative wear involving copper tape and/or conductive fabric/thread, LED lights, batteries, switches, and crafts	• How to build parallel circuits • How to incorporate snap switches
Light-up Trinkets & Bulleten Boards	Paris, KJ, JK	Creating light-up boards and objects for displaying pictures, accomplishments, and anything else	• How to build parallel circuits • How to creatively design switches with crafts
Canvas Art	Tim, Luke, Kim	Painting canvas (small and medium-sized) with light-up components	• How to build parallel circuits • How to incorporate light schemes into art
Soldering	Samuel, Mac	Practicing how to solder; soldering their artifacts made at other stations	• How to solder circuit connections
Multi-meters and Renewable Energy	Jasmine	Learning how to use a multi-meter to determine power requirements of artifacts produced and voltage production of renewable energy sources	• How to use multi-meters to determine power demands of a circuit • How to measure voltage produced by batteries and by renewable energy sources (e.g., hand-crank generators
Hot Glue and Other Tools	Fall	Introducing participants to a range of tools used in their makerspace to prepare for the event, and to support participants in modifying their designs	• How to use common tools in making in traditional and nontraditional ways (e.g., making a phone case out of hot glue)
Snacks and Chill Zone	Wolf, Fall	Hanging out when either the youth leaders or the participants needed a break from the workshop	• How to share ideas and how to deal with frustration

7–8) at the club. Martha, the assistant director of the community club, had selected a "junior mentee" each for the youth. The youth, young mentees, four adult mentors, and Martha all watched the movies that the youth had made earlier in the semester. Nine stop-motion movies were shown that the youth had made over a 3-month period (see Table 7.2 for descriptions of the movies). The stories that were told ranged from fantasy to issues youth experienced at school, such as bullying and making friends, to what youth appreciated about being at the community club.

After the nine movies were shown, the young mentees and adults applauded the youth makers. When an adult mentor asked the junior mentees what materials their older peers used in their movies, they were quick to raise their hands and chorus out the answers: Playdough! Paper! Toys! People! The young mentees were eager to start building their characters with the materials laid out. Once they were paired up with a maker youth leader, each pair or group got to work.

In preparing for the workshop, the youth spent 8 weeks in the fall learning how to make stop-motion movies using the iPad. None of the youth had ever done this before. The youth investigated YouTube videos of others' stop-motion movies to get ideas, including videos involving characters made of two-dimensional paper drawings, three-dimensional playdough figurines, and persons themselves. With the help of adult mentors the youth also explored different apps on their iPad for making stop-motion animations. They investigated green screens and green props such as green felt, gloves made of green felt, and homemade plastic pipe props on which to drape the green felt for green screen work (to help with making more sophisticated stop-motion animations). Then, using these skills and tools, along with a wide range of toy figurines, LEGOs, playdough, and miscellaneous arts and crafts supplies, such as popsicle sticks and pipe cleaners, the youth spent a significant amount of time constructing their own movies. They visited a local university's makerspace three times during this period, where they had access to more materials and received feedback from the maker-mentors there about their projects. Youth learned how to manipulate different features of the stop-motion app, including automated picture taking, slowing down frames, editing footage, and audio functions.

EXPANDING MAKER-ROLES, EXPANDING AGENCY

We selected these two cases because they reflect different ways of thinking about and responding to how youth sought to expand their own and others' agency to make toward the public good, and in how their actions sometimes resisted and recreated expectations (thereby changing the norms and power structures) for making within their community.

Table 7.2. Stop-Motion Movies

	Movie (made by)	Synopsis (written by youth)	Materials Used/Features
1	*Back to School Troubles* (Dan and Don)	This story is about how school is boring . . . sometimes there is bullying but the boys end up being friends.	Youth themselves, peer at the club, and adult staff member at the club recruited to act as teacher; club premises
2	*Dimensions of Pac-Man* (Soul and Keenan)	3 short stories about Pac-Man: • From enemies to friends • Big Pac-Man and little Pac-Man • Pac-Man revolution	Youth used following materials to make Pac-Man figures: • Construction paper • Playdough • LEGOs Green screen features on app Searched, saved, and imported Pac-Man game background for green screen work
3	*Flower on a White-board* (Kat, with help from adult mentor)	How to draw a beautiful flower on a whiteboard	Whiteboard, whiteboard markers of different colors, Kat's drawing skills
4	*Revenge of the Bunny* (Jan)	This movie is about a bunny feeling un-wanted, so she wants to get revenge on the other animals that are innocent.	Toy figurines, green screen features on app. Jan searched, saved, and imported two different backgrounds for green screen work, one forest scene and one laboratory scene
5	*The Adventures of Blue and Yellow Guy at the Boys and Girls Club* (Dan and Don)	Two creatures, Blue and Yellow Guys, play games and hang out at the Boys and Girls Club	Created playdough figurines—blue and yellow guys, and accessories such as a puck for the characters to play hockey with using the air-hockey table, used furniture/spaces at the community club

Table 7.2. Stop-Motion Movies (continued)

	Movie (made by)	Synopsis (written by youth)	Materials Used/Features
6	*The Dance Life* (Kat and Seneca)	How two girls enjoy dancing and being at the Boys and Girls club	Girls themselves posing in many different ways to make up a stop-motion dance; locale of community club
7	*The First Day of School* (Alice and Shona)	How two girls met at school in 4th grade at [local] Christian Academy	Plastic doll figurines, popsicle sticks, beads, other found objects that girls made into furniture for the classroom, including a blackboard, teacher's desk with computer, books, and papers, and a student's desk with a beaker and exploding scientific experiment
8	*The Magical Horn* (Dan and Diana)	Animals that are in the forest . . . and a blue man comes and blows a horn, and the king comes, and they bow, then eat and they go to sleep, and wake up flying, they flew because of the horn, then they fly	Toy figurines, green straws, green glove for moving toy figurines, popsicle sticks for building other props Green screen features on app. Youth searched, saved, and imported a background for green screen work
9	*War on the Creatora* (Josh)	A person created evil robots, but one got away, ten years later the creator captured a princess	Toy figurines, green screen features on app. Josh searched, saved, and imported a futuristic forest background for green screen work

Though the electric art workshop was designed to invite anyone of any age at their club to their makerspace, the stop-motion movie workshop was a focused workshop for a small number of younger students, who were paired one-on-one with current youth makers. The electric art workshop focused on teaching others about energy and circuitry and supporting others in making material artifacts they could take home and use in ways they wished. The stop-motion movie workshop focused on teaching digital fabrication of virtual artifacts that could be shared broadly online.

Despite these differences, we see powerful parallels in these youth-led efforts to expand participation in making into their community. In what follows we describe four expansive community youth maker *practices* that emerged in their efforts: (1) developing their own (and providing opportunities for others to develop) STEM-rich making knowledge and practice in accessible and salient ways; (2) supporting participants, via youth-authored pedagogy, in (a) exploring ideas/practices, (b) feeling accomplished, and (c) creating things that matter; (3) designing structures and artifacts for enhancing visibility and discourse of making within the community; and (4) Promoting critical consciousness of STEM access, opportunity, and engagement.

We describe how these practices took shape, and show how they worked toward moments of remaking STEM-rich making. We argue that these practices support an iterative and generative process of authoring rightful presence and place-making, allowing for restructuring positional and knowledge hierarchies among community, students, teachers, and science—conditions necessary for moments of equitable and consequential making. As youth designed and enacted their workshops, they authored a rightful presence for youth makers—both themselves and their invited peers, who solve community problems in age-appropriate ways. At the same time, they engaged in place-making: seeding the cultural norm for the community youth making space to have this practice/value, in which more porous boundaries between communities and STEM-rich making are produced.

Developing and Extending STEM Expertise

The youth sought to design creative ways to extend their learning and to encourage other youth to engage with STEM-rich making knowledge and practices in accessible and salient ways. What we see as important here is that this process involved both an attention to one's own experiences making as well as a leveraging of community insights to projects (and negotiating in the moment) that others may need to make in ways that matter.

Across both workshops, youth spent significant time over weeks and months developing both their STEM knowledge and maker practices, which they drew on to help their peers have the same successes they had had in making.

Take for example, Kim, a 13-year-old veteran maker, who had been in her maker club for 2 years. As she prepared for the event, she designed several different electric art cards and worked with the canvas to get ideas for what other kids might make, and how they might do so. However, this process for Kim was frustrating:

> I was frustrated about it, though. When I was doing mine, when I finally joined in, the thing I worked really hard on wasn't lighting up like I wanted it to. It was the canvas art, the galaxy with some of the LED lights in it. I feel like I finally did it. [Then I helped] by asking questions, 'cause, like, there were some kids . . . and they were having trouble and I was telling them [how to do it]. Say they were wondering how the light lights up and they couldn't get it to light up. I would just help them and make sure their circuit was complete and not just all mumbo-jumbo.

Kim noted how hard she worked on her own project, and how she felt when she could not get her galaxy design to light up on her canvas. Her frustration, however, became a source of inspiration for her in considering what challenges and frustrations her younger peers may have. She thought about what questions to ask them. She wanted her peers to figure out how their light-up canvas actually worked, and not be, in her words, "mumbo-jumbo."

The goal of the canvas art station that Kim helped design was to support participants in doing more advanced circuitry in combination with their art. Because the canvases were larger than the other trinkets at other stations (e.g., mini bulletin boards), participants could add multiple lights to the canvas, requiring a parallel circuit if it is to be lit by a single 3V battery. The youth leaders at this station were concerned with how complicated electric art can be, and they wanted to provide a space for their peers to work through more challenging problems.

The canvas station was one of two stations held in the official makerspace room (the other was a second soldering station). This was a conscious decision on the part of Kim and the other youth leading the workshop. They wanted to ensure that when people painted, they would have enough space to do so. They did not want people accidentally bumping into wet paint, and the canvases took up more space than the other activities.

In designing this station, the youth created several different example canvases with different circuits for participants to glean ideas from. They had a poster explaining how to make a canvas. The youth and the one adult working at the station sat at the table working on their own art or helping others as they joined in.

For Kim and for many of the other youth, this act of knowing what it was like firsthand to learn these skills and then to teach them to others was important because, as she stated, "It's important to teach kids, like, what's going on in the world. How to engineer, like, say if they need help with something to fix, that they'll end up fixing it themselves without asking any help."

However, learning the STEM skills for successful light-up art was not the sole focus. The dialogue around the table focused on the art itself. The youth leaders asked the participants about who the art was for and what it meant for the young people who made it. At one point in the evening, a young girl was making an anti-bullying canvas that she wanted to hang up at school. She said, "This light-up sign says 'no bullying.' The lights will help people pay attention to it." Other youth made art to give away to their parent or guardian. As one young man said, "I made this for my mom. It has a heart and a flower. I know she will love it."

Furthermore, though all of the stations ran differently—different youth, different activities—underlying each station was a clear dedication to ensuring that their peers had opportunities to make things for themselves, and to have the time and the space to learn the skills they needed to do that.

Take, for example, Mac's efforts at the soldering station. At any given moment he could be found involved in an exchange like the following between Mac and a participating youth:

Mac: Do you have your copper tape? Okay, okay you're going to want to put a piece of copper tape here. Like this.

Mac then demonstrated on his own piece of construction paper.

Mac: Okay you do it. (Waits about 35 seconds while the young girl attaches copper tape to her project.)
So this is where the light comes in. You are going to want to put a piece of copper tape here like this.

Mac then demonstrated again on his own piece of construction paper, and urged his participant to try it on her own: "Okay, you do it." After he watched the girl work on affixing the tape over about 45 seconds, he moved on to how to affix the lights: "And then take the light and do this," again demonstrating. At each step in the process, from assembling the initial circuit, to using the soldering gun, he carefully modeled for his participants how to do each step of the process, then patiently waited while they figured out how to do it with their own hands.

I'm gonna make him do as much of the pushing buttons as possible. In the stop-motion animation workshop, we get a glimpse of how the youth leaders had to develop a suite of expertise over time in order to run their workshop. As part of this they had to learn how to combine their expertise in creative ways in order to design their movies and workshop activities.

Thirteen-year-old Keenan started at the home page of the iPad and showed Jay the stop-motion app icon. He asked Jay, 8 years old, to touch the icon "to open the app." Keenan seemed to be checking back at the "how to teach" steps that the youth had collectively decided on earlier in the session, before the younger mentees arrived. The steps were written on the whiteboard in the making space.

Keenan leaned over to the adult mentor watching and said, "I'm gonna make him do as much of the pushing buttons as possible." Turning to Jay, he continued the conversation:

Keenan: What do you want your movie to be about?
Jay: About two monsters fighting . . . playing.
Keenan: Okay. Where do you want them to fight, or play?
Jay: I want to use the game tables outside . . . can we use the game tables outside?

Keenan momentarily turned to an adult mentor to ask permission to go into the common area of the club where the game tables are because he wanted to "take a picture of the game table." As the two boys moved around the games room, Keenan carefully showed Jay how to take a picture of the foosball game console by positioning the iPad at a particular height so as to get the desired size of the game table, and he showed the importance of keeping the iPad stable when taking the picture. The boys then took a picture of the air-hockey table.

When they returned to the making space, Keenan showed Jay the icons on the stop-motion app and asked Jay to touch certain icons to select for "green screen mode" and then another icon near the bottom of the screen to "import the background." After importing each background in turn into the stop-motion app and seeing how it would appear on the screen (Jay pressing the buttons with Keenan watching), Keenan discovered that the proportion of the background was "off" and would not work with the proportion of the playdough creatures that Jay was building. Keenan had run into the exact same problem when he was making his third Pac-Man stop motion movie. The first two Pac-Man game backgrounds he had saved and imported were "off" in proportion. He had to find a third one that would work with the size of his Pac-Man figure.

While Jay built his two characters out of playdough, Keenan, a talented artist, helped him with some of the finer details, such as spikes on the creature's back. He showed Jay how to roll out a thin piece of playdough and then use a ruler to flatten out one end. Jay told the adult mentor: "I'm making two creatures, two monsters. This one will have all these blue spikes." At the same time, Keenan also searched online for

Figure 7.2. Keenan's Whiteboard Steps

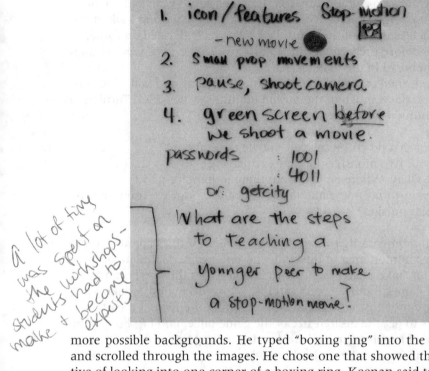

1. icon / features   Stop-Motion
   — new movie
2. Small prop movements
3. pause, shoot camera
4. green screen before
   we shoot a movie.
   passwords   : 1001
               : 4011
   or: getcity

   What are the steps
        to teaching a
        younger peer to make
   a stop-motion movie!

a lot of time was spent on the workshops — students had to become make + experts

more possible backgrounds. He typed "boxing ring" into the search bar and scrolled through the images. He chose one that showed the perspective of looking into one corner of a boxing ring. Keenan said to the adult mentor, "This will work with his characters fighting. The ring will be behind them." Keenan also showed Jay what he had found and made sure Jay liked the background chosen.

Jay, with help from Keenan, set up a green screen stage by taping green construction paper together and using playdough containers as a support (see Figure 7.3). Keenan made sure that the stage they constructed had enough green paper to be the "stage floor" of the background. With Keenan's help and suggestions, Jay moved the characters slowly while Keenan held the iPad steady. Jay would move the creatures, and then push the button to take a picture, with Keenan holding the iPad as steady as possible. After a few shots, Keenan showed Jay the timed picture-taking function and suggested they set the timer so Jay could focus on just moving the characters, and Keenan would hold the iPad steady. They worked this way until the end of the session. During the process, Keenan helped Jay create dents and frowns on the character that was losing the fight.

In preparing for both community workshops, youth spent significant time engaging in making activities with their peers, which built their

Figure 7.3. Keenan and Jay Working on Props

peers' expertise with specific making tools and practices. In the case of the stop-motion moviemaking, the youth were introduced to an app, and through making/using the app, increasingly learned more features of the app, as described above. The level of detail in the making of props evolved over time as the youth grew more competent, developed more skills, and grew more confident. Sixth-graders Alice and Shona built very detailed props for their stop-motion movie. They took into consideration the scale of the books and lamp that would sit on the teacher's table that they built. In the case of the electric art, the youth prototyped different activities, deciding on the ones they felt were most interesting and durable for younger peers to make and bring home. In the process, they also figured out other possible challenges their peers might face when engaging in their projects. For the youth in the making programs, this consistent, long-term access to making experiences, and the multifaceted aspects of becoming both expert makers and maker-mentors to peers, is a marked departure from the transient, "keychain" approach critiqued by some maker scholars (Blikstein & Worsley, 2016).

Youth-Driven Pedagogical Approaches

While the examples above illustrate the suite of knowledge and practices the youth leaders sought to teach others, we want to turn our attention to the youth-driven pedagogical approaches they chose to do so. We saw in the case of the electric canvas art that Kim based her pedagogical touch on the challenges she personally faced in her own electric art efforts. She purposefully spent time thinking about what problems she had so that she would be ready to help others with those problems. Likewise, Keenan had Jay working hands-on at each step, even when that meant having to get permission to move around the club to take pictures or slowing down the process of importing photos into the app because Keenan felt Jay should do that himself.

We observed that many of these pedagogical approaches played the dual role of helping their participants explore maker ideas and practices while also ensuring that they felt—and were acknowledged as—"accomplished" in the process. For example, at the stop motion workshop, the exemplar movies showed included characters that were made of playdough, but some were three-dimensional and some two-dimensional. The youth discussed the different camera positionings their mentees would have to maintain with 3-D versus 2-D characters. They engaged their mentees in conversation about "tradeoffs"—2-D characters are easier to make, but you need to hold the camera directly overhead and keep that steady, which is very tiring (based on youth makers' own experiences). We share more extended examples of youth-driven pedagogical approaches in what follows.

Multi-meters by Jasmine. Take this extended example of "Multi-meters with Jasmine." Jasmine's station at the electric art event focused on teaching youth about producing electricity from hand cranks and measuring the voltage with multi-meters. (Hand-crank generators are small, portable devices that transform kinetic energy from turning a hand crank into electrical energy.) A vibrant 6th-grader, Jasmine volunteered to run this station because "no one else wanted to." During the planning session other youth eagerly volunteered for the more "fun" stations like soldering or making wristbands or cards. However, Jasmine said she did not mind taking over this station because it was important. In her words, "You have to understand how it works so that you can use it to make things."

On the day of the workshop, a handmade poster hung behind her table with large colorful letters that read, "Multi-meters by Jasmine." Several hand cranks sat on the table, with two multi-meters in the center. A game she made with copper tape, LED lights, and construction paper sat in the middle. As Jasmine reported, "Today at my station, I taught everyone about multi-meters, which are right here, and I taught them how to use a hand crank. I taught them how hand cranks can make voltage like a battery, and I showed them how to measure it on the multi-meter to let them know what amount of energy they could have."

Jasmine creatively set up the need for renewable energy sources by keeping a bin of used and worn-out batteries at her table. She could demonstrate that worn-out batteries had limited to no voltage and that the hand crank would always generate voltage so long as one was using it. In fact, at any given moment, Jasmine could be found describing how hand cranks and multi-meters work, and helping the young people who visited her station use these tools on their own. She insisted that visitors test things out for themselves, and challenge themselves to think about different possibilities for these tools. As she stated, "I also had them demonstrate for themselves how to use the hand crank, and to crank it hard to see how many voltages they could get to."

With the skill of a veteran teacher, Jasmine anticipated the challenges that her visitors may have reading the multi-meter and interpreting the numbers. She offered suggestions for how her visitors might manipulate the tools to figure things out on their own when they seemed stuck or confused. Take for example, what occurred about midway through the evening. Six youth (four boys and two girls) stood around her table. Jasmine had just handed a hand crank to one of the youth, and said: "Try going really fast. See how many volts you can get!" As the boy turned the crank slowly, she patiently waited. She then took the multi-meter, which was attached to the hand crank, and pointed to the display, and said to the group, "So you can see he has under one volt!"

Jasmine then took the hand crank from the youth and handed it to another, with the following exchange:

Jasmine: Okay, you want to try now?
Girl: [Nods her head yes]
Jasmine: Okay, see how it [the multi-meter reading] went down? It's because it [hand-crank motor] stopped spinning! Okay, you try now.

As the girls started to work the hand crank, Jasmine again pointed to the multi-meter reading and said:

Okay, so you can see she also has a little under one volt. See how that is. See the gear inside? When you are pushing on this, it will spin that, which is what is making the energy. These wires go connected to the multi-meter so you can see how much energy you just made. Someone want to try? Go really fast? Watch!

As Jasmine worked the hand crank as fast as she could, the youth at her table became animated, calling out the numbers on the hand crank, exclaiming, "You got 19 voltages!"

Jasmine then took the game she made, and showed everyone at her table how you could use a multi-meter to see if the circuit was closed. The game (see Figure 7.4) was built on a piece of orange construction paper

Figure 7.4. Jasmine's Electricity Game

with four images of familiar objects on the right (green grass, blue bike, red apple, and purple paint), and color splotches on the left (red, green, blue, and purple). Connected to each image was a strip of copper tape and a second piece of flapping copper tape. Hidden on the back of the paper were the completed copper tape circuits connecting the appropriate color with the image and a battery. The goal of the game was for the player to connect the correct color with the image by connecting the flapping pieces of tape to the tape next to the image. When done correctly, the circuit would complete and the light would go on.

Jasmine said she made the game at the "last minute" with materials around her making space because she wanted to have a way for the "little kids" to be interested in circuits. She also thought that the older kids might find the game useful for figuring out "more complicated ideas" like "how to use multi-meters."

At the end of the evening, she noted that she "learned about what people know about what voltage is. I was glad I got to teach people different things. I also learned that you have to make sure that the negative and positive leads of whatever you are using to connect it are not touching, but if you don't, it won't work because it's connected" (thereby creating a short circuit). When we asked her about the game she made for her station, she said, "I want to be able to make something that will help people and will be encouraging to others to do better things and to be able to make things that teach others how to do awesome things like we do in [our club]."

Prepped what they would say

Prepping to be maker-mentors to peers. Preparing for their events required the youth to mull over a wide range of considerations. Figuring out how to help others with technically challenging aspects of electric art was a common theme in the youth's preparations. Earlier, we noted that Jasmine spent extra time making her circuit game to help make circuits easier for little kids. We also noted that Kim paid attention to the things that were frustrating for her so that she could help other kids who might have the same frustrations.

Sydney, in her comments below, illustrates how she spent time "prepping what to say" about how feeling frustrated is something that they all have experienced.

I was prepping for, like, what I would say to them, and if some would be interested or let them in a little bit of secrets about how hard it was and stuff like that. And then that's how I figured out how to make it light up. It was a very hard process because I had, I had worked for, like, 3 days trying to get it to work, when finally, on, like, the maybe 7th day I got it to work, and I was really happy, but only one lit up instead of all five. It was really hard.

[I had to think about how to say] like, this is like copper tape and if you put a battery on it, and a light on it, it will most likely light up. The side you have it on is really important there. Positive and negative. And then I prepped, like, if you guys are—it took me a really long time to do this and here's what I had to go through, too.

Other electric art workshop stations followed similar patterns but focused on different electric art activities. At the wristband station— renamed mid-workshop by one of the youth from bracelets to wristbands to engage the boys—the youth had two large posters calling attention to the station, with images and text offering ideas on how to make their art. They wore examples of different kinds of wristbands they made to show off the technology and to encourage the interest of others. They had laid out the materials needed to make light-up wristbands across the table so that many kids could take up the task at once.

The youth also had to consider, out of the possibilities inherent in a making project, what to prioritize. With the stop-motion app workshop, youth leaders considered the range of features available that could be explored, once a decent-length movie is made with a substantial number of photographs taken (at least 60 to 80). There were options to insert different theme cards, record dialogue, and other audio options. Out of all the features, youth leaders decided the green screen option was the most interesting, and that they would focus on that one. Dan reminded the group that the "[mentees] still have to build their characters with playdough and backgrounds . . . and they want to have a movie done." These pedagogical decisions, to fit the constraints of a 75-minute workshop, were based on the youths' own experiences as they learned how to use the stop-motion moviemaker app over several weeks.

Translating maker practices and expertise to peers. While working on his stop-motion movies, Keenan created Pac-Man characters during different materials. He drew Pac-Man characters on yellow construction paper with different facial expressions. He made playdough Pac-Man characters and also LEGO Pac-Man characters. With the LEGO Pac-Man, Keenan searched online for YouTube videos that showed how pieces can be staggered to create curves. When he moved on to green screen work, he learned how to search for and import backgrounds, play with the sensitivity function to determine degree of visibility for his characters vis-à-vis the background. His expanding expertise took time to develop, through multiple sessions of making with the stop-motion app. He had made three different stop-motion movies before coaching Jay at the Big Brother, Big Sister stop-motion workshop.

Keenan's expertise translated into the agency he displayed during his coaching. He made sure to show Jay where the different function buttons are located in the app, and when to press which button. He showed Jay how to take background pictures when Jay wanted to use the green screen function, and helped Jay do it himself. When the chosen pictures of the game consoles did not work with how Jay was creating his playdough characters, Keenan checked in with the adult mentor and proceeded to search online for a background that would work with Jay's storyline and that would give a realistic perspective to the figures in a boxing ring. He brought his expertise to helping Jay create a realistic and aesthetically pleasing scenario for Jay's stop-motion story. When Jay played his movie, he was delighted, and pronounced it "COOL!" When asked if he enjoyed the workshop, Jay said, "Yes, I really like it. Can I come back again?" Many of the younger mentees expressed similar sentiments.

Designing Structures and Artifacts

As youth considered what they wanted to teach and how they might teach it, they drew upon their experiences to produce a set of structures and artifacts that resulted in the enhanced visibility and discourse of making within the community. Although youth may not have purposefully sought to create structures, we see their efforts resulting in new possibilities for extending the reach of their makerspace temporally and spatially in ways that opened new connections between their making space and youth and community.

First, youth sought to help their peers make things that they could carry with them beyond the workshop, either materially or virtually. One of the youth leaders also noted that later, when walking around the club after the event, dozens of youth were seen still sporting their wristbands. She said that was "cool" because "it showed everyone that they could do it, too." Having these real reminders of their accomplishments was important to the youth because they wanted their peers to have others "see" what they made, and to be recognized for it. In fact, one of the adult mentors noted that the wristband station was especially popular, and that the wristbands had "a lot of social cachet among both youth leaders and all the little kids who came in . . . everyone wanted one."

It was further important because they wanted these artifacts to have deeper meaning in their lives. In the example above involving the canvas station, the youth were excited to support their peers in making signs that would prevent bullying and projects to give to their parents or guardians. As one of the youth leaders, Tara, reflected on the canvas station, "I really liked the art that the kids made. They kept making it for so many different people . . . My favorite ones were the ones that had messages on it, like 'You can do it' and like 'stop bullying.' I think we helped the other kids have things to say in creative ways."

Second, we see the sharing of tools and knowledge as vitally important especially as it relates to how the visitors felt welcomed in these spaces. If we return to the Stop-Motion Animation workshop, we saw that all the youth leaders not only helped the mentees with learning how to use the app itself, but they also showed techniques and gave tips to the mentees, drawn from their own experiences, on how to create characters out of playdough and other materials. Youth leaders also improvised with materials in the making space, such as using a plastic crate and boxes to elevate the iPad to the required height so that mentees could capture particular scenes the way they envisioned. Sharing such connected expertise that included all aspects necessary to make a stop-motion movie goes far beyond understanding how the app worked. It is necessary to literally create the story as well. Youth leaders made sure to help their mentees in all the related aspects, in whichever way mentees wanted to begin (you could choose to work with playdough to make the characters first, or you could play around with the app first, or design the backgrounds). Once their movies were made, the mentees were excited to show the movies to their friends in their age group in the club, and to their parents and club staff members.

In short, we believe that the practice of designing structures and artifacts resulted in enhanced visibility and discourse of making within the community but also increased porosity between the making space and the community—helping work toward a connected and collective culture of making.

Promoting Critical Consciousness of STEM Access, Opportunity, and Engagement

We begin this section with Kim's reflections on her work in the electric art workshop, about 2 months after the event:

> *Researcher:* What do you think this design says about you?
>
> *Kim:* I feel like it, like, represents me. Not only am I a girl but I can work hard to get something done in such a short amount of time.
>
> *Researcher:* Can you tell me more about what it says about you as a girl?
>
> *Kim:* Um, *I feel like it kinda shows that I'm a girl that won't stop trying*—I don't wanna listen to people; I wanna try doing it my own way.
>
> *Researcher:* So your own way. Why is that important?
>
> *Kim:* Because if you have people telling you what to do, like, and your passion isn't what they're telling you to do and you wanna do it—you wanna do something but you're being told to do something else—if you do it by yourself you'll be able to do what you wanted to do and not have anyone telling you how to do it, or what you're doing.

Having the opportunity to design and lead these workshops led many of the youth to critically reflect on what the experience meant to them, and why that was important. In this opening quote, Kim is challenging gendered norms in making—"I feel like it kinda shows that I'm a girl that won't stop trying."

Her sentiments, however, are echoed in the expectations and scaffolds they brought to the workshop for others. They wanted their peers, girls and youth of color, to have success in making, to not have it appear as "mumbo-jumbo," and to have durable and usable artifacts to bring home and share with others. These explicit and implicit messages about who can make and what it means to make were a part of the workshop tapestry. Ariel reflected, "I can't believe I can teach someone to do something. . . . I helped Junior (mentee) make a stop motion movie."

Promoting a critical consciousness of STEM access, opportunity, and engagement also meant using the workshop to open up new opportunities for their peers. As Shona best explained when asked if she and the other youth would be willing to host a similar event again:

It is good to show what we can do and share that with other kids who are not in [our club]. It's good for the little kids, too. . . . Of course they spent their time better here with us than their regular whatever it is they do. They got to learn how to make a stop motion movie! They got to use technology and create and make something fun!

What Shona brought up was important in how the youth are framing how their making program can serve others in their community. The younger children typically have homework time and then time in the gym. Sometimes a movie is put on for them to watch, especially during the holiday season. There were not many existing opportunities to "use technology and create and make something fun." At the same time, hosting these community events where they explicitly share their newly gained making expertise was empowering for the youth. Ariel, a very shy youth leader who usually professed doubts about her abilities, was in disbelief about how well the event went for her and her younger mentee. She said to an adult mentor, "I can't believe I taught someone how to do something!"

Similar sentiments were expressed by youth in the electric art workshop, as they reflected on how their workshop made their makerspace "as big as the community." For example, when asked after the workshop what she was most proud of, one of the youth, Tara, said, "I cannot believe how many kids came. We taught them about electric art, and they got to bring their projects home to decorate their rooms. I felt like we kind of make our maker club as big as the community. Everywhere you look and see electric art, you can think that is what we do."

Table 7.3 below summarizes the robust nature of the STEM knowledge, maker technique know-how, associated making expertise, and positive making experience that the youth maker leaders shared with the peers in their community.

Toward a Culture of Equitable and Consequential Making

The stories shared in this chapter showed how the youth worked to make in ways that extended and transformed accessibility: interactive workshop activities that directly involved youth in maker activities, maker activities with direct links to the community, opportunities to make things to bring home or do something with, providing tools and resources for making changes, and juxtaposing serious messages with playfulness. For these strategies to be effective, resources—structural, human, and material—that already resided within these communities were called into play. It was a concerted community effort, even as the planning for these events were largely youth-led.

As the youth sought to expand and transform the places of making through enacting the practices highlighted in Table 7.3, they did so in ways that intersected the physical, cultural, and social identities that defined their making space and its ongoing evolution. That is, they

Table 7.3. Community Youth Maker Practices

	Stop-Motion Animation	Electric Art
STEM-rich maker knowledge and maker project–specific knowledge	Proportion/scale of characters to background Calculating number of pictures per second, 100 pictures for 1 minute of film Learning particular features of the app, such as the green screen feature, importing and adjusting the sensitivity of backgrounds relative to characters	Components of a circuit (load, power source, switch, and conductor) Types of circuits: simple, series, parallel Measurement: power requirements, voltage Soldering Power tools
Pedagogies for enacting hybrid knowledge and practice	Leveraging making skills developed from other projects to help mentees create characters and props	Studying one's own challenges and addressing those in teaching primarily through storytelling Using own and peers' projects as exemplars Locating activities within sociohistorical contexts Laughing, playing, and having fun with participants
Structures and artifacts	Showing their own movies as examples during the workshop Movies shown as part of "club happenings" on the front lobby TV	Wearing art projects throughout the various spaces of the club throughout the evening and beyond Displaying youth art throughout the club Producing take-home artifacts that you can give to loved ones
Critical consciousness	Youth maker leaders express importance for sharing making opportunities with younger peers	Discussing the opportunities and challenges of making within workshop tables Talking about the workshop as a tool for expanding making into the community Referring to participants as youth makers and experts

sought to extend their own rightful presence in making, and open up opportunities for others to have such a presence as well. In their workshops, they sought to remake narratives on how STEM-rich knowledge and practices might be leveraged—including the forms they take and how they are used—toward the public good. They capitalized on local community assets (e.g., larger lobby spaces in the community club where different age groups of peers and parents mingle) and potentialities (e.g., open community club events they co-opted to host making workshops), resulting in a set of experiences that contributed to greater access and participation in STEM-rich making in the moment, but also projecting forward. It was not enough for the youth to simply offer an enjoyable experience with an artifact for one to take home. The youth sought to ensure that the ideas and practices brought to the workshops by their peers became a part of their efforts to help their peers deepen and extend their STEM knowledge and practice. STEM-rich making had to involve more than "mumbo-jumbo."

This dialectic—ensuring both an enjoyable and robust making experience—appears critical to sustaining equitable and consequential making for youth. However, this dialectic needs to be cultivated. Community-based and participatory forms of research/activity were central to the youth's practice, as they iteratively moved and repurposed ideas, tools, and practices across and within their community and makerspace.

In each of the practices above, we see how the youth draw upon their insider status, positioning themselves as legitimate community members as they sought to figure out what activities may be enjoyable and how so, or how to respond to the challenges they encounter. Just as important, these practices were deeply interactive, taking shape through interaction with community members, thereby coproducing new narratives of who a maker is or can be. These interactions also were not completely new. The youth, being insiders, repurposed existing structures within the communities, such as "Big Brother Big Sister events" where expert, adult outsiders are invited in to take on the roles of big sister and big brother in teaching the club youth some skills. Instead of being the recipients of mentorship from outsiders, the youth makers positioned themselves as the big sisters and big brothers to teach stop-motion movie how-to to younger peers.

LOOKING AHEAD

Across the two workshops, the youth desired to create making spaces that were inviting to members of their community and that were fundamentally participatory. We want to caution that it would be easy to "singularly responsibilize" their efforts to suggest that it was their responsibility to generate new narratives for making/making spaces for their community, rather than consider the ways in which their work was only made as richly possible *by working with community* (e.g., Bain & Landau, 2017). This was the youth's grassroots approach to seeding, in collaboration with community, what they collectively determined to be a community- and youth-centered making culture.

To respond to Lee and colleagues' (2015) critique regarding the lack of details on what exactly happens when taking a grassroots metaphoric approach to frame the spreading of the maker movement, we suggest that the stories shared here show how the seeding and spreading of a community- and youth-focused making culture could potentially unfold, answering the questions of "how the 'grass' has been placed, whether it was started as seed or sod, why it took hold, how it spread, and what it needed in order to grow" (p. 2). The youth sought to spread access and opportunity in making with and in their community in ways that were grounded in their lives and sociohistorical context. They created events that were filled with playfulness, enjoyment, and entertainment. They supported others in engaging in making activities that carried importance in their lives, and that could travel with them physically and virtually beyond the workshop. They desired to teach their community about making (using STEM knowledge of circuitry, green energy ideas and practices, digital stop-motion moviemaking) in an environment that blurred boundaries between STEM, making, communities, and everyday concerns. The youth's movement across communities allowed for new forms of making that foregrounded collective responsibility and the public good as essential to both the learning and doing of makers.

CHAPTER 8

Making and the Equity Agenda
Looking Forward

During the semester when the youth makers were working on building toys for children in their community, they spent several sessions making Styrofoam toy cars. This was due in part to youth's own interest in creating toy cars as gifts for children, as well as an opportunity to learn how to safely use maker tools and widen their making expertise. They learned how to use an electric hot-wire cutter to carve the car bodies out of foam. They shaped their cars to make them more aerodynamic with different grades of sandpaper. They tested how far apart on the body of the car to space the plastic wheels and axle. Collaboratively, the youth also built a cardboard racetrack to test their cars on, indicating where the starting line should be and how steep the incline of the track should be.

In researching their cars, the youth created different designs. Sasha and Tallie made their foam car in the shape of a unicorn, as both girls liked unicorns. As Sasha described, "You can make your car whatever you want. We like unicorns, so ours is a unicorn. When we build cars, we can be as girly as we want to be." Sasha's Styrofoam unicorn was decorated with paint and rainbow glitter. Kayla made her car in the shape of a letter K, for her name, because, as she said, "This is MY car." Keenan painstakingly used two different grades of sandpaper to shape triangular pieces—"wings"—to attach to a sleek, angled body with hidden toothpicks.

After 3 weeks of building, testing, and refining, including building a racetrack out of corrugated cardboard, the youth had a final competition on the racetrack, to see whose car would go the farthest. They held the contest in the common community area of the club, and many of the other youth, who are not in the making club, watched their contest with interest and enthusiasm.

After the session, the youth makers decided that they wanted to leave their cars and racetrack in the common area for a week, and invite friends at the club to play with the cars and "test them out." Sharon suggested that their peers "can test the cars, and write a note to tell us which one they liked." A few of the youth, including Sharon, then set up the racecars, racetrack, and Post-it notes on a table in the common area (Figure 8.1). Throughout the week, the youth makers observed, to see if other peers tried out the cars. Two club staff members told

Figure 8.1. Race car and Track

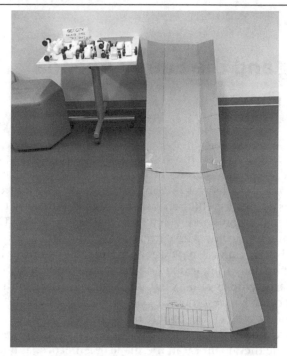

Figure 8.2. Sharing Race cars with Others

maker-mentors that the "race cars were a hit with the kids the whole week! The smiles! Many of the kids asked if they could also join [making club] and make their own cars." Some children left Post-it notes that read, "COOL CARS!" and "FUN!!" The club staff members took pictures of the children playing with the cars throughout the week and shared them with the youth makers. When we met the following week at our regular making session, youth enthusiastically reported that "Kids played with the cars every day the whole week!" and "Every day that I was here and in the lobby I see kids playing with the cars," and "Miss Martha showed us pictures of the other kids playing," and "It makes me feel good to make the cars and see other kids play [with them]." Many youth makers reflected strong sentiments of pride and joy at being able to share their creations with other children at their community club. Sasha noted, "It makes a difference that *we* made the cars. *We* made them at our [making club]." The youth makers then decided that they would request a similar setup and share the cars and racetrack at another community event later in the year (Figure 8.2).

EQUITABLE AND CONSEQUENTIAL STEM-RICH MAKING AND MAKER LEARNING

We begin with this vignette to call attention to the kinds of making experiences we believe are both equitable and consequential, and the program design principles that may make such forms of making possible in community-centered making spaces. Recall that by equitable and consequential, we refer to (a) experiences that provide empowering opportunities for students to engage with the knowledge and practice of STEM-rich making in culturally sustaining (i.e., valuing the expertise and experiences youth bring to learning) and rigorous ways, and (b) how such opportunities toward advance disciplinary learning promote transformative outcomes aimed at addressing systemic inequalities, such as critical agency, educated action, and social transformations.

When we consider what may be equitable and consequential, we think it is important to consider the forms of engagement, the practices engendered by these forms, and the outcomes of youth's making efforts. We will unpack these main points using the Styrofoam toy car vignette and other examples introduced across the book in the text below and end the chapter with an illustration of these points in Figure 8.3.

Equitable and Consequential Forms of Engagement

If we return to the Styrofoam toy car vignette, we can think about how engagement takes shape across space and time. We note, in particular,

Figure 8.3. Equitably Consequential Making in Community

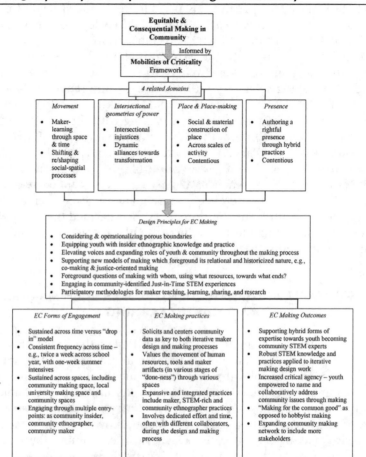

that the *frequency and range of "access" and "opportunity" youth makers had were both consistent and wide.* Across the stories shared in this text, youth makers have access to twice-a-week making sessions at their community club, each session lasting 90 or more minutes. They have access to tools and materials necessary for the explorative nature of their making. In the car vignette, youth engaged in a making activity of their choice across several sessions, related to their larger goal of making toys for children in their community, or for younger peers at their community club, even as adult mentors suggested learning how to make Styrofoam cars as a possible choice. Further, what could easily have been a 1- or 2-day affair stretched over weeks as youth sought to make more complex car designs, in shapes and with properties that personalized the cars for them. They also sought to expand from cars to a racetrack so that other children in the club could enjoy the toys they made.

leads to multiple entry points

We also note the *making occurred across many different spaces*. Many of the youth makers worked on aspects of their projects at home, in other locations of the club, and in various places in the community as they engaged in dialogue with others on their projects (an important part of making) or as they sought to get feedback on how their project may work for others. As we see with the cars (similar to the electric art and the stop-motion movie events shared in Chapter 7), the youth purposefully designed to take their making projects into the broader space of the club. As the other children played with their toys, they tweaked the toys so that they would continue to work, and they also shared their experiences with others through the toys, playful banter, and talk. *Not only does this expand where making happens, but it also opened up multiple entry points to making.* For some youth, the making itself is the motivation (whether it's the technical or aesthetic dimensions), but for others it is the desire to do things for others, to be social with friends, or to have a chance to be recognized by others, among other points of entry.

Furthermore, embedded within such access, they have opportunities to learn and develop making expertise with a range of tools and materials, including opportunities to deepen their STEM knowledge. Across our studies, youth learned and explored a wide range of challenging but necessary STEM knowledge and practice, through just-in-time STEM activities, in order to have their designs work in the ways they wished. Whether it was figuring out complex circuits to power a light-up scooter, testing the heat capacity of different heating elements for a heated boot, learning how to weight lights and batteries on a football to ensure proper aerodynamics, or learning how to layer data in GIS maps, the youth increased their exposure to the knowledge, practices, and technicalities of these domains as they sought to make. For example, in the vignette above, youth learned through the design of racecars the relationship between sleekness of the car body and speed. They explored how to design and conduct a fair test, and the need to conduct more than one trial to take an average reading. They consulted relevant sources of information, iteratively designed and made and explored how to test one independent variable at a time, be it setting the wheels farther apart, using longer or shorter axles, or changing the shape of the car body.

As we saw across the projects, these STEM-related domains include but are not limited to the following:

- Electronics: Standard circuits, paper circuits, e-textiles (all involve simple, series, and parallel circuits; power requirements, loads/outputs, switches)
- Thermodynamics: Heat, insulation, and relationship to work/energy
- Renewable energy: Power sources, energy production, energy transformations

- Measurement: Angles, lengths, weight
- Materials: Properties and uses of materials
- Forces and motion: Push/pull, gravity, aerodynamic features
- Health and bodies
- Ecosystems
- Weather and climate
- Programming and digital skills: App building, Arduino programming, 3-D digital sketching
- GIS mapping: Inputting and layering data, big data
- Survey analysis
- Fair test conditions and analysis

While we do not make claims about "how much" the youth learned in these areas, we do believe that the stories of their making presented across these chapters offer evidence that they dug into these topics in ways that went beyond school learning.

Additionally, the nature of access and opportunity differs both in degree and in kind between community makerspace experiences and the stand-alone, "drop-in" making experiences that typically mark school excursions to museums or libraries with making programs. Though such drop-in experiences could very well be significant in catalyzing interest in making for some youth, we argue that access that is grounded in consistency, frequency, and range in making experiences is one essential way to support youth makers in establishing a rightful presence in making. Further, the deep and sustained nature of such access and opportunity in community is the foundation on which youth makers can learn to be—true to who they are when they are making, that is, not take on imposed identities—and to become youth makers of consequence in their communities. As a result of the sustained nature of their making, youth developed a range of making expertise and competency with a range of making tools. They were then able to use these tools for later projects.

Equitable and Consequential Making Practices

Opportunities for sustained engagement with others, across spaces and over time, make it possible for youth to engage in a suite of making practices that expand their opportunities to engage in STEM-rich making.

As youth were supported in *soliciting and centering community data as key to both iterative maker design and making processes*, they learned to see the problems they wished to solve as larger than themselves. They also gained access to *new ideas, tools, and experiences shared by others* toward making sense of the problems they wanted to solve and in generating potential solutions. In the car vignette, youth drew upon their experiences broadly at home and in the club to make note that more opportunities for youth to play with toys was a valuable activity. Youth also used their peers' experiences playing with the toys to tweak their models so that the children would have greater fun.

We have seen these same kinds of movement across the stories shared in this text. Fall and Samuel drew extensively on their research into the local library and bus system; interviews and surveys with peers, parents, and other adults; and their own experiences to craft their Little Free STEM Library project. And when Samuel used the paper circuit kit they put in the library to show other kids how it worked by making a light-up card, he produced a video on his successes where he shows his electric art card lighting, with him narrating in the background, "Look at me, guys! I am so smart! It's lighting up! I never knew circuits like this before." He put the video on Facebook to encourage his wide groups of friends and acquaintances to come to the Little Free STEM Library.

In this example, as in others, it is not only the centering of community data or movement of experiences that transforms the making process, it is the way these *ideas, tools, and experiences expand and integrate into more traditional maker practices, recreating what it may mean to make.* The stories in this text are rich with examples of the many hybrid forms of practice youth authored toward making. Powerful here is not only that new practices develop that promote new forms of expertise among youth, but also how those forms of expertise are rooted in the wisdom of lives lived in community in ways that push back against multiple dominant narratives about whose knowledge and experiences count and why. When Christopher worked on his anti-bully app, he purposefully crowdsourced his community through a feature on his app to help further identify kinds of bullying (physical, verbal, etc.), and plot specific locations of instances on a map, and the days and times one might encounter them. When Kairee and Jaida wished to find ways to help riders and drivers in the public transportation system stay warm, they rode the different bus routes—which they have been riding "since we were babies cuz our mom drives the number [x] bus"—taking careful notes and surveying riders and drivers about their experiences. As these examples also show, these new and varied hybrid practices involve *dedicated effort and time, often with different collaborators, during the design and making process.*

Equitable and Consequential Making Outcomes

We believe that the equity-oriented nature of the making experiences described above informed consequential impacts of making experiences, and vice versa, in a positive feedback loop. We further conjecture that it is through youth makers engaging in this mutually reinforcing mode of equitable and consequential making that their agency to engage in place-making toward a rightful presence as community youth makers grows; they can then advocate for other youth at their community club to share in these experiences. As they experience equitable and consequential making experiences themselves, youth makers begin to advocate for equitable and consequential making experiences for others in their community, through sharing their innovations (e.g., toy car), to hosting maker events to intentionally teach other children at the club how to make (e.g., events described in Chapter 7).

When considering consequentiality in making, we note that the outcomes of making are related to the four elements of the Mobilities of Criticality framework—movement, intersectional geometries of power, place-making, and presence—and how they intersect toward transformative outcomes aimed at addressing systemic inequalities. The transformative outcomes that youth makers have collectively displayed include the development and manifestation of critical agency and educated action (in making and hosting maker workshops for the public good) toward social transformation (restructuring knowledge and power hierarchies in terms of making culture and interactional norms at the community club).

We can think of critical agency in STEM-rich making as using STEM-rich maker knowledge and other forms of distributed expertise to take action to redress instances of injustice. While it is important for youth to be supported in developing the agency to make in ways that matter in their lives, we think it is equally important that their agency helped restructure knowledge and authority hierarchy in the making community. In many ways, the kinds of critically oriented making that the youth took up were about more than simply solving problems that mattered in their community (although this is important); they also made connections between local issues they identified and systemic patterns of injustice. From careful documentation of food and library deserts; to access to games, toys, clothes, and accessories; to the recording of the stories of lives lived in creative digital formats, the youth sought to belong in making, with their whole lives, and with their collective wisdom, to push back against the injustices they have experienced. As we shared in Chapter 3, when youth authored their own "Makerspace Manifesto," they made public and highly visible the message that a making space is "a place where you can invent, have fun, and make stuff to save the world."

We argue that these modes of consequentiality work in concert to support youth in engaging in place-making toward establishing a rightful presence as community youth makers. They support the youth in their leadership roles as they recruit community stakeholders during the making process, and as they teach and curate making experiences for other youth in the community clubs. In the car vignette above, how the youth designed their cars and why revealed the movement of ideas and resources drawn from other experiences as well as the intersectional geometries of power, especially those of gendered norms in the context of building racecars, intersecting with what counts as creative, authentic, equity-oriented making. As evidenced by the variety of car designs, youth makers were not constrained to the gendered norms often taken as default in STEM-related experiences. Unicorn- and alphabet-shaped racecars were made alongside more traditional racecar models. Washi tape, paint, and glitter were among the materials used by youth to decorate their race cars in whatever ways they chose. Although these decisions may seem small and mundane (and indeed they are), we are reminded that systemic injustices are often insidiously perpetuated through the small and mundane, and that seemingly pedestrian acts of decisionmaking can, in fact, hold great potency in reclaiming one's space and authority in empowering ways.

We do not conflate equity-in-making with the notion of equality defined as "fairness" or "one size fits all," as implied by the distributive views of justice. Replicating the models of making programs built on dominant maker culture norms, even if they are outfitted with all the sophisticated tools typically found in these spaces, we argue, would not be veridical toward creating an authentic, empowering community making space with nondominant youth. In fact, we argue the opposite—simply importing a White, male, middle-class model of a making program would serve to further alienate youth of color from making, in effect denying them a rightful presence by demanding that they become the other. As youth makers Kayla and Ivy have reminded us, youth need to feel that they are wanted in the making spaces, and that they have a different perspective from adult makers about what a youth-focused making space needs to feel, look, and sound like. Assuming "free and open access to all" simply because a sign at a public library making space indicates it as so neglects the fact that oppression often manifests in silent and prosaic ways. The presence of an "atmospheric wall" can be equal to its brick-and-mortar cousin in keeping out less privileged "others" through signaling a message of alienation and trespassing.

Foregrounding youth's relationality in community is a productive way to break through such atmospheric walls. Through the stories of youth making in, with, and for community shared throughout this book, we have striven to show that the processes youth collaboratively undertook, with support from adult mentors, in establishing a rightful presence at the community club with their making work, served to seed and solidify cultural norms and practices of the community making space, a making culture that is uniquely their own. Indeed, the actions that the youth—across our stories—have taken involve their *enacting new practices that seed the emerging culture of the community making space.* We see this in how the youth in the opening vignette moved the cars out into the common area in the club and invited other children at the club to play with the toys and leave feedback. However, we also see this in how the youth sought to bring their communities into their making projects, to create a place for their voices and experiences to matter.

Indeed, the youth engaged in *place-making* at the club through the movement of their made artifacts (e.g., toy cars and racetrack) from the making space room to the large common lobby area. The practice of moving made artifacts out of the making space into community added another dimension to the consequentiality of the youth's making experiences that is connected to scales of activity. Youth toymakers engaged in a robust STEM-rich process of making the race cars. Through sharing the toys with the community at the club, the youth expanded the scale of their activity, providing entertainment and exploration opportunities to their younger peers. This sharing is also grounded in relationality. The older youth makers are friends with many of the younger ones, and had them in mind as recipients of other toys they would eventually make. Through these moves, youth makers were authoring a rightful presence for themselves, and for those they make for, at the community club.

The recognition that youth makers received through sharing their made artifacts with the community conferred added consequentiality to their making while also affirming their identities as community makers. The youth felt "accomplished," as Fall described in her blog post, that they had made something they were proud of and that had rigor and personal ownership. Youth makers also positioned themselves as community maker-mentors through sharing their made artifacts and hosting making workshops for their younger peers. These activities served to recruit younger peers for whom they can be role models in the making space. These practices all work toward seeding an authentic, community-based, youth-driven making culture.

COCREATING AN EMERGENT, COMMUNITY-FOCUSED YOUTH MAKING CULTURE WITH YOUTH MAKERS

Place-Making Toward Rightful Presence Within Community Is Dynamic and Contentious

Both our making spaces reside in community clubs that have long served low-income youth and youth of color in empowering ways. Programs committed to helping youth include daily homework support, sports development, and opportunities to develop leadership skills, such as in the Girl Scout program. At one of the sites, the community club reached out to the local ballet company, which partnered with them by sending a volunteer dancer once a week to teach young club members (ages 5 to 8) ballet. We believe that partnering with the community clubs helped immensely in situating the making program "on youth's and community's turf" from the start. Since youth already spend significant after-school time at the community club, many of the concerns regarding physical access to the making program were mitigated. We conjecture that with the making space situated at the community club, where youth already spend significant time and where most have a personal history and connection (understanding its norms and practices, being positioned as cherished youth members of the club), these nodes of historicity and relationality also translated in tangible ways to the community club staff. Members of the staff could be supportive of the new ways in which youth engaged in further place-making in the club, as youth makers sought to expand the boundaries of community making. For example, we see how youth, by moving their artifacts into a common area and creating a sustained opportunity for younger peers to test the cars and interact with the made artifacts, engaged in place-making in two ways—club common space became a physical and interactive space with STEM-oriented, age-appropriate activities accessible to all in that space; place-making for the youth makers who have embedded their presence and what they can offer through making embraced the larger club space. Positioning themselves with new roles as youth maker-mentors and teachers when novel opportunities related to making opened up, the youth illustrate the dialectical nature of place-making (e.g., Ma & Munter, 2014) between youth, the physical spaces of the community club, and how the youth interacted in those spaces both socially and materially. The youth that larger societal narratives have considered problematic—youth of color from low-income backgrounds—are now the embodied experts and resources in the community (Taylor, 2017) for equitable and consequential making.

However, place-making toward a rightful presence is not free from tension. As Gruenewald (2003) reminds us, "[p]eople make places and places make people" (p. 621). Even as both community clubs genuinely care for and are supportive of their youth members, the tendency to defer to the market models of STEM and making remain, especially when there is no established model of a community youth making space where youth and community members are stakeholders throughout the making process. Coupled with the community clubs' goals to provide the youth they serve with robust programs aimed at improving character and academic outcomes, was our commitment to spending time supporting youth in figuring out the contours of an authentic community youth making space. As university partners and adult mentors, we have had to advocate on behalf of the youth and take on the role of "go-between" to broker for particular place-making opportunities, such as hosting a community event that featured making workshops. The fact that we have to broker implies that even when youth are "on their turf" at the community club, they do not necessarily have unfettered leeway to freely place-make toward rightful presence.

Related to this point, we conjecture that as adults, club staff/mentors themselves have differing views of what a rightful presence as makers at a community club entails, especially if the dominant maker culture is held as the standard. Community club staff members who had visited our university making spaces voiced much admiration for these professional spaces and the kinds of projects in progress there. There seemed to be an assumption, however, that such a space (and its attendant practices) could be neatly imported into the community club, with youth undertaking similar kinds of projects. Such an assumption reminds us of how systemic oppressions are also mobile—they move from space to space, even to spaces that value the youth, like the community clubs. When we think about movement, as in the youth moving of resources and made artifacts in and out of spaces, we acknowledge that oppressive practices can also move when they are imported as seemingly mundane "best practices" and "gold standards" with the best intentions.

However, as we have discussed in the previous chapters, youth themselves construed rightful presence in markedly different ways. How youth frame and consider rightful presence as community youth makers is related to their experiences of the intersectional geometries of power. As youth of color from low socioeconomic backgrounds, their experiences along intersecting axes of oppression (e.g., being Black and female; being homeless; being Black, male, and in multigenerational poverty) precipitated challenging realities in their everyday lives that impact how they engage with the world across spaces. The youth's rejection of a "wholesale" import of making spaces they visited reflects their understanding of how they view systemic injustices meted out along these oppressive axes, and their desire to counter the injustices. As a result, youth's engagement in place-making toward rightful presence on their own turf, in a community space, is still necessarily political.

Considerations for Equitable and Consequential Making Design Principles

Lastly, we have sought to elucidate program design principles for building such empowering making spaces with youth in community.

We began this book with concerns about how the dominant culture in the maker movement has paid little attention to exploring a range of making experiences with diverse youth makers. Seeking *a range of making experiences* necessitates broadening the boundaries that define making and makers, often in ways not yet imagined, because we are bound to "depart from the text" of the maker canon in seeking equitable and consequential making experiences for youth in community.

We suggest new ways of looking at youth maker learning when both equity and consequentiality of the making experiences are considered as *non-negotiables*. Expanding what counts as community youth maker practices has been productive in helping us identify when and how making experiences can move toward deeper equity and consequentiality for the youth makers and their community. The equitable and consequential making practices listed in Figure 8.3 share as a common denominator youths' rootedness in their communities. Both the making processes and the made artifacts themselves are embodied manifestations of the youths' existing and developing knowledge of their communities: STEM and making woven together toward critical justice–oriented making. These ways of making lead to equitable and consequential making outcomes characterized by expanding boundaries of the making community that legitimizes expansive forms of making expertise. These ways of making also equip youth with robust STEM knowledge and practices in culturally and socially responsive ways and support their development of critical agency, positioning them as capable of helping solve community challenges through making.

We end this book with hope that the maker movement will indeed steadily expand its culture to not only be inclusive of historically marginalized youth; we hope the maker culture will unapologetically position all youth to make toward a better world for themselves and their communities.

The youth makers themselves are hopeful. We leave you with their words:

> At maker club, you can get hands-on about making. You can dare to be extraordinary. You can inspire young thinkers. At our maker club, we are technical thinkers. We can make our dreams a reality, and make to help our community solve problems and become even better.
> —Liza (12 years old), Tonya (11 years old), and Sasha (11 years old) talking about their community making club

> I feel like it will be super cool. People will love it. They'll say, "Who made this?" It was me. Then they'll ask me like, "The tiny person always in the background did this?" I'll say, "Yeah, I did that. . . . Little kids can do ginormous work!"
> —Jennifer, 11-year-old maker

References

Alper, M., Hourcade, J. P., & Gilutz, S. (2012). Adding reinforced corners: Designing technologies for children with disabilities. *interactions, 14*(6), 72–75.

American Society for Engineering Education [ASEE]. (2016). *Envisioning the future of the maker movement: Summit report.* Retrieved from www.asee.org/documents/papers-and-publications/papers/maker-summit-report.pdf

Bain, A. L., & Landau, F. (2017). Artists, temporality, and the governance of collaborative place-making. *Urban Affairs Review,* 1078087417711044.

Balibar, E., Mezzadra, S., & Samaddar, R. (2012). *The borders of justice.* Philadelphia, PA: Temple University Press.

Bang, M., & Bajaras, F. (in press). Towards Indigenous making and sharing: Claywork in an Indigenous STEAM program. *Equity & Excellence in Education.*

Bang, M., & Medin, D. (2010). Cultural processes in science education: Supporting the navigation of multiple epistemologies. *Science Education, 94*(6), 1008–1026.

Bang, M., Marin, A., Faber, L., & Suzukovich III, E. S. (2013). Repatriating indigenous technologies in an urban Indian community. *Urban Education, 48*(5), 705–733.

Barnett, C. (2005). The consolations of "neoliberalism." *Geoforum, 36*(1), 7–12.

Bautista, M. A., Bertrand, M., Morrell, E., Scorza, D. A., & Matthews, C. (2013). Participatory action research and city youth: Methodological insights from the Council of Youth Research. *Teachers College Record, 115*(10), 1–23.

Birtchnell, T., & Urry, J. (2013). 3D, SF and the future. *Futures, 50,* 25–34.

Blikstein, P., & Worsley, M. (2016). Children are not hackers: Building a culture of powerful ideas, deep learning and equity in the maker movement. In K. Peppler, E. Halvorsen, & Y. Kafai (Eds.), *Makeology: Makerspaces as Learning Environments* (Vol. 1, pp. 64–80). New York, NY: Routledge.

Brahms, L., & Crowley, K. (2016). Learning to make in museums. The role of maker educators. In K. Peppler, E. Halvorsen., & Y. Kafai (Eds.), *Makeology: Makerspaces as learning environments,* (Vol. 1, pp. 15–29). New York, NY: Routledge.

Bright, N., Manchester, H., & Allendyke, S. (2013). Space, place, and social justice in education: Growing a bigger entanglement. *Qualitative Inquiry, 19*(10) 747–755.

Buchholz, B., Shively, K., Peppler, K., & Wohlwend, K. (2014). Hands on, hands off: Gendered access in crafting and electronics practices. *Mind, Culture, and Activity, 21*(4), 278–297.

Calabrese Barton, A., & Tan, E. (2009). Funds of knowledge and discourses and hybrid space. *Journal of Research in Science Teaching, 46*(1), 50–73.

Calabrese Barton, A., & Tan, E. (2010). We be burnin'!: Agency, identity and learning in a green energy program. *Journal of the Learning Sciences, 19*(2), 187–229.

Cammarota, J., & Fine, M. (Eds.). (2008). *Revolutionizing education: Youth participatory action research in motion.* New York, NY: Routledge.

Cole, M., Kaptelinin, V., Nardi, B., & Vadeboncoeur, J. A. (2016). Scale, agency, and relationships: The work of cultural-historical and activity theoretical research. *Mind, Culture and Activity, 23*(2), 93–94.

Crenshaw, K. (1991). Mapping the margins: Intersectionality, identity politics, and violence against women of color. *Stanford Law Review, 43*(6), 1241–1299.

Cresswell, T. (2014). *Place: An introduction.* New York, NY: John Wiley & Sons.

Cresswell, T. (1996). *In place/out of place: Geography, ideology, and transgression.* Minneapolis, MN: University of Minnesota Press.

Dawson, E. (2014). "Not designed for us": How science museums and science centers socially exclude low-income, minority ethnic groups. *Science education, 98*(6), 981–1008.

DiGiacomo, D. K., & Gutiérrez, K. D. (2016). Relational equity as a design tool within making and tinkering activities. *Mind, Culture, and Activity, 23*(2), 141–153.

Dougherty, D. (2011, January). *We are makers* [Video file]. Retrieved from https://www.ted.com/speakers/dale_dougherty

Duffy, D., & Bailey, S. (2010, June). *Whose voice is speaking? Ethnography, pedagogy and dominance in research with children and young people.* Paper presented at Oxford Ethnography Conference, Oxford, England.

Duncan-Andrade, J. M. R., & Morrell, E. (2008). *The art of critical pedagogy: Possibilities for moving from theory to practice in urban schools.* New York, NY: Peter Lang.

Eckert, J. (2016). Beyond Agatha Christie: Relationality and critique in anthropological theory. *Anthropological Theory, 16*(2–3), 241–248.

Eisenhart, M. A., & Finkel, E. (1998). *Women's science: Learning and succeeding from the margins.* Chicago, IL: University of Chicago Press.

Engeström, Y., & Sannino, A. (2010). Studies of expansive learning: Foundations, findings and future challenges. *Educational Research Review, 5*(1), 1–24.

Erickson, F. (1984). What makes school ethnography "ethnographic"? *Anthropology & Education Quarterly, 15*(1), 51–66.

Fendler, R. (2013). Becoming-Learner: Coordinates for mapping the space and subject of nomadic pedagogy. *Qualitative Inquiry, 19*(10), 786–793.

Fine, M. (2008). An epilogue, of sorts. In J. Cammarota & M. Fine (Eds.), *Revolutionizing education: Youth participatory action research in motion* (pp. 213–234). New York, NY: Routledge.

Freire, P. (1970). *Pedagogy of the oppressed.* New York, NY: Continuum.

Friedmann, J. (2007). Reflections on place and place-making in the cities of China. *International Journal of Urban and Regional Research, 31*(2), 257–279.

Gonzales, L. D., & Terosky, A. L. (2016). From the faculty perspective: Defining, earning, and maintaining legitimacy across academia. *Teachers College Record, 118*(7), 1–44.

González, N., Moll, L. C., & Amanti, C. (Eds.). (2006). *Funds of knowledge: Theorizing practices in households, communities, and classrooms.* New York, NY: Routledge Press.

Gray, A. (2002). *Research practice for cultural studies.* London, England: Sage.

Green, T. L. (2015). Places of inequality, places of possibility: Mapping "opportunity in geography" across urban school-communities. *Urban Review, 47*(4), 717–741.

Gruenewald, D. A. (2003). Foundations of place: A multidisciplinary framework for place-conscious education. *American Educational Research Journal, 40*(3), 619–654.

Gruenwald, D. A., & Smith, G. A. (Eds.). (2008). *Place-based education in the global age.* New York, NY: Taylor & Francis.

Gutiérrez, K. D. (2008). Developing a sociocritical literacy in the third space. *Reading Research Quarterly, 43*(2), 148–164.

Gutiérrez, K. D. (2012). Re-mediating current activity for the future. *Mind, Culture, and Activity, 19*(1), 17–21.

Gutiérrez, K. D., & Rogoff, B. (2003). Cultural ways of learning: Individual traits or repertoires of practice. *Educational Researcher, 32*(5), 19–25.

Halverson, E., & Sheridan, K. M. (2014). The maker movement in education. *Harvard Educational Review, 84*(4), 495–504.

Hawkins, D. (1974). *The informed vision: Essays on learning and human nature.* New York, NY: Agathon Press.

Hayano, D. (1979). Auto-ethnography: Paradigms, problems, and prospects. *Human Organization, 38*(1), 99–104.

Heath, S. B. (2012). Seeing our way into learning science in informal environments. In W. F. Tate (Ed.), *Research on schools, neighborhoods, and communities: Toward civic responsibility* (pp. 249–267). New York, NY: Rowman & Littlefield.

Holland, D., & Lave, J. (2001). *History in person: Enduring struggles, contentious practice, intimate identities.* Santa Fe, NM: SAR Press.

Holland, D., & Lave, J. (2009). Social practice theory and the historical production of persons. *Actio: An International Journal of Human Activity Theory, 2,* 1–15.

Holland, J. (2015). Bursting with ideas. *Vision: Maker movement,* (pp. 127–131). Retrieved from https://www.jessicaeholland.com/s/Makerspace.pdf

Honneth, A., & Fraser, N. (2003) *Redistribution or recognition? A political-philosophical exchange.* London, UK: Verso.

Hyrapiet, S., & Greiner, A. L. (2012). Calcutta's hand-pulled rickshaws: Cultural politics and place making in a globalizing city. *Geographical Review, 102*(4), 407–426.

Jenkins, H. (2006). *Confronting the challenges of participatory culture: Media education for the 21st century.* An occasional paper on digital media and learning, John D. and Catherine T. MacArthur Foundation. Retrieved from https://www.macfound.org/media/article_pdfs/JENKINS_WHITE_PAPER.PDF

Johnson, A., Brown, J., Carlone, H., & Cuevas, A. K. (2011). Authoring identity amidst the treacherous terrain of science: A multiracial feminist examination of the journeys of three women of color in science. *Journal of Research in Science Teaching, 48*(4), 339–366.

Jones, P., & Evans, J. (2012). Rescue geography: Place making, affect and regeneration. *Urban Studies, 49*(11), 2315–2330.

Jurow, S., & Shea, M. (2015). Learning in equity-oriented scale making projects. *Journal of Learning Sciences, 24*(2), 286–307.

Kafai, Y. B., Fields, D. A., & Searle, K. A. (2014). Electronic textiles as disruptive designs: Supporting and challenging maker activities in schools. *Harvard Educational Review, 84*(4), 532–556.

Kafai, Y. B., Peppler, K. A., & Chapman, R. N. (2009). *The computer clubhouse: Constructionism and creativity in youth communities.* New York, NY: Teachers College Press.

Keune, A., Gomoll, A., & Peppler, K. (2015, September 26–27). *Flexibility to learn: Material artifacts in makerspaces.* Paper presented at the fifth annual FabLearn Conference: Equity and Diversity in Making. Palo Alto, CA: Stanford University.

Lave, J., & Wenger, E. (1991). *Situated learning: Legitimate peripheral participation.* Cambridge, MA: Cambridge University Press.

Leander, K., Phillips, N., & Taylor, K. (2010). The changing social spaces of learning: Mapping new mobilities. *Review of Research in Education, 34*, 329–394.

Lee, V. R., King, W. L., & Cain, R. (2015). *Grassroots or returning to one's roots? Unpacking the inception of a youth-focused community makerspace.* Instructional Technology and Learning Sciences Faculty Publications. Paper 510. Retrieved from https://digitalcommons.usu.edu/itls_facpub/510

Lewis, C. (2012). Oppositional culture and educational opportunity. *School Field, 10*(2), 131–154.

Lombard, M. (2013). Citizen participation in urban governance in the context of democratization: Evidence from low-income neighbourhoods in Mexico. *International Journal of Urban and Regional Research, 37*(1), 135–150.

Lombard, M. (2014). Constructing ordinary places: Place-making in urban informal settlements in Mexico. *Progress in Planning, 94*, 1–53.

Ma, J. Y., & Munter, C. (2014). The spatial production of learning opportunities in skateboard parks. *Mind, Culture, and Activity, 21*(3), 238–258.

Maker Media. (2013). Retrieved from makermedia.com/wp-content/uploads/2014/10/impact-of-the-maker-movement.pdf

Martin, L. (2015). The promise of the maker movement for education. *Journal of Pre-College Engineering Education Research, 5*(1), Article 4. Retrieved from http://dx.doi.org/10.7771/2157-9288.1099

Massey, D. (2005). *For space.* London, England: Sage.

Moll, C., Neff, D., & Gonzalez, N. (1992). Funds of knowledge for teaching: Using a qualitative approach to connect homes and classrooms. *Theory Into Practice, 31*(2), 132–141.

Morrell, E. (2006). Youth-initiated research as a tool for advocacy and change in urban schools. In S. Ginwright, P. Noguera, & J. Cammarota (Eds.), *Beyond resistance!* (pp. 111–128). New York, NY: Routledge.

Nasir, N. I. S. (2011). *Racialized identities: Race and achievement among African American youth.* Palo Alto, CA. Stanford University Press.

Nasir, N. I. S., Rosebery, A. S., Warren, B., & Lee, C. D. (2014). Learning as a cultural process: Achieving equity through diversity. In K. Sawyer (Ed.), *The Cambridge handbook of the learning sciences* (2nd ed, pp. 686–706). New York, NY: Cambridge University Press.

Nascimento, S., & Pólvora, A. (2016). Maker cultures and the prospects for technological action. *Science and Engineering Ethics*, 1–20.

Nash, J. C. (2008). Re-thinking intersectionality. *Feminist Review, 89*(1), 1–15.

National Academy of Engineering. (2010). *Engineering, social justice, and sustainable community development.* Washington, DC: National Academies Press.

National Research Council. (2010). *Engineering, social justice, and sustainable community development: Summary of a workshop.* Washington, DC: National Academies Press.

National Science Foundation. (2014). *Science & Engineering Indicators 2014.* Retrieved from http://www.nsf.gov/statistics/seind14/content/etc/nsb1401.pdf

NGSS Lead States. (2013). *Next generation science standards: For states, by states.* Washington, DC: The National Academies Press.

Norris, A. (2014). Make-her-spaces as hybrid places: Designing and resisting self constructions in urban classrooms. *Equity & Excellence in Education, 47*(1), 63–77.

Ozer, E. J. (2016). Youth-led participatory action research. In L. Jason & D. Glenwick (Eds.), *Handbook of methodological approaches to community-based research: Qualitative, quantitative, and mixed methods* (pp. 263–272). New York, NY: Oxford University Press.

Peppler, K. (Ed.) (2017). *The SAGE encyclopedia of out-of-school learning.* Los Angeles, CA: Sage Publications.

Peppler, K. A., & Bender, S. (2013). Maker movement spreads innovation one project at a time. *Phi Delta Kappan, 95*(3), 22–27.

Peppler, K., Halverson, E., & Kafai, Y. B. (Eds.). (2016). *Makeology: Makerspaces as learning environments* (Vol. 1). New York, NY: Routledge.

Perumal, J. (2015). Critical pedagogies of place: Educators' personal and professional experiences of social (in)justice. *Teaching and Teacher Education, 45*, 25–32.

Rahm, J. (2014). Reframing research on informal teaching and learning in science: Comments and commentary at the heart of a new vision for the field. *Journal of Research in Science Teaching, 51*(3), 395–406.

Ratto, M. (2011). Critical making: Conceptual and material studies in technology and social life. *The Information Society, 27*(4), 252–260.

Ratto, M., & Boler, M. (Eds.). (2014). *DIY citizenship: Critical making and social media.* MIT Press.

Rawls, J. (1971). *A theory of justice.* Cambridge, MA: Harvard University.

Relph, E. (1976). *Place and Placelessness.* London, England: Pion Limited.

Rios, D., Bowling, M., & Harris, J. (2016). Decentering student "uniqueness" in lessons about intersectionality. In K. Case (Ed.), *Intersectional pedagogy: Complicating identity and social justice* (pp. 194–213). New York, NY: Routledge.

Rodríguez, L. F., & Brown, T. M. (2009). From voice to agency: Guiding principles for participatory action research with youth. *New Directions for Student Leadership, 2009*(123), 19–34.

Roth, W. M. (2008). Constructing community health and safety. In *Proceedings of the Institution of Civil Engineers-Municipal Engineer 161*(2), 83–92. London, England: Thomas Telford Services.

Rubel, L. H., Hall-Wieckert, M., & Lim, V. Y. (2017). Making space for place: Mapping tools and practices to teach for spatial justice. *Journal of the Learning Sciences, 26*(4), 643–687.

Ryoo, J. J., Bulalacao, N., Kekelis, L., McLeod, E., & Henriquez, B. (2015, September). *Tinkering with "failure": Equity, learning, and the iterative design process.* Paper presented at FabLearn 2015 Conference at Stanford University.

Said, E. W. (1989). Representing the colonized: Anthropology's interlocutors. *Critical Inquiry, 15*(2), 205–225.

Sato, T. C. (2013). *Examining how youth of color engage youth participatory action research to interrogate racism in their science experiences.* Unpublished dissertation, Michigan State University.

Schlosberg, D. (2013). Theorising environmental justice: The expanding sphere of a discourse. *Environmental Politics, 22*(1), 37–55. DOI:10.1080/09644016. 2013.755387

Schmidt, R., Chen, V., Gmeiner, T., & Ratto, M. (2015, July). 3D-printed prosthetics for the developing world. In Proceedings of *SIGGRAPH 2015: Studio* (p. 21). ACM.

Schrock, A. R. (2014). "Education in disguise": Culture of a hacker and maker space. *InterActions: UCLA Journal of Education and Information Studies, 10*(1).

Shea, P. (2016). Civic practices, design, and makerspaces. In A. McCosker, S. Vivienne, & A. Johns (Eds.), *Negotiating digital citizenship: Control, contest and culture,* (pp. 231–246). London, England: Rowman & Littlefield.

Sheridan, K. M., Halverson, E. R., Litts, B. K., Brahms, L., Jacobs-Priebe, L., & Owens, T. (2014). Learning in the making: A comparative case study of three makerspaces. *Harvard Educational Review, 84*(4), 505–531.

Sheridan, K. M., & Konopasky, A. (2016). Designing for resourcefulness. In K. Peppler, E. Halverson, & Y. Kafai (Eds.), *Makeology: Makerspaces as learning environments* (pp. 30–46). New York, NY: Routledge.

Simpson, A. (2007). On ethnographic refusal: Indigeneity, "voice" and colonial citizenship. *Junctures: The Journal for Thematic Dialogue,* (9), 67–80.

Smith, A. (2015). *U.S. smartphone use in 2015.* Pew Research Center, 1.

Squire, V., & Darling, J. (2013). The "minor" politics of rightful presence: Justice and relationality in *City of Sanctuary. International Political Sociology, 7*(1), 59–74.

Squire, V. (2009, July). *Mobile solidarities: The City of Sanctuary movement and the Strangers into Citizens campaign.* Report of findings of the Open University's Pavis

Research Project. Retrieved from http://www.open.ac.uk/ccig/sites/www. open.ac.uk.ccig/files/Squire%20Mobile%20Solidarities%20report%20_3_. pdf oro.open.ac.uk

Taylor, K. H. (2017). Learning along lines: Locative literacies for reading and writing the city. *Journal of the Learning Sciences, 26*(4), 533–574. doi:10.1080/ 10508406.2017.130719.

Taylor, K. H., & Hall, R. (2013). Counter-mapping the neighborhood on bicycles: Mobilizing youth to reimagine the city. *Technology, Knowledge and Learning, 18*(1–2), 65–93.

Tedlock, B. (1991). From participant observation to the observation of participation: The emergence of narrative ethnography. *Journal of Anthropological Research, 47*(1), 69–94.

Trueba, H. T. (1999). Latinos Unidos: From cultural diversity to the politics of solidarity. Lanham, MD: Rowman & Littlefield.

Tuan, Y.-F. (1977/2001). *Space and place: The perspective of experience.* Minneapolis, MN: University of Minnesota Press.

Tuck, E. (2009). Suspending damage: A letter to communities. *Harvard Educational Review, 79*(3), 409–428.

Tzou, C., Scalone, G., & Bell, P. (2010). The role of environmental narratives and social positioning in how place gets constructed for and by youth. *Equity & Excellence in Education, 43*(1), 105–119.

Unterhalter, E. (2012). Mutable meanings: Gender equality in education and international rights frameworks. *Equal Rights Review, 8,* 67–84. Retrieved from https://opendocs.ids.ac.uk/opendocs/handle/123456789/12757

Vossoughi, S., Escudé, M., Kong, F., & Hooper, P. (2013). *Tinkering, learning, and equity in the after-school setting.* FABlearn Conference Proceedings. Palo Alto, CA: Stanford University.

Vossoughi, S., & Gutiérrez, K. (2014). Studying movement, hybridity, and change: Toward a multi-sited sensibility for research on learning across contexts and borders. *National Society for the Study of Education, 113*(2), 603–632.

Vossoughi, S., Hooper, P. K., & Escudé, M. (2016). Making through the lens of culture and power: Toward transformative visions for educational equity. *Harvard Educational Review, 86*(2), 206–232.

Vrasti, W., & Dayal, S. (2016). Cityzenship: Rightful presence and the urban commons. *Citizenship Studies, 20*(8), 994–1011.

Watson, A., & Till, K. E. (2010). Ethnography and participant observation. In D. DeLyser, S. Herbert, S. Aitken, M. Crang, & L. McDowell (Eds.), *The Sage handbook of qualitative geography* (pp. 121–137). Thousand Oaks, CA: Sage.

Yoder, B. (2014). Engineering by the numbers. American Society for Engineering Education. Retrieved from https://www.asee.org/papers-and-publications/ publications/college-profiles/15EngineeringbytheNumbersPart1.pdf

Yosso, T. J. (2005). Whose culture has capital? A critical race theory discussion of community cultural wealth. *Race, Ethnicity and Education, 8*(1), 69–91.

Young, I. (1990). *Justice and the politics of difference.* Princeton, NJ: Princeton University Press.

Zeldin, S. (2004). Youth as agents of adult and community development: Mapping the processes and outcomes of youth engaged in organizational governance. *Applied Developmental Science, 8*(2), 75–90.

Index

About the Authors

Angela Calabrese Barton is a professor in teacher education and science education at Michigan State University. She has a PhD in curriculum, teaching and educational Policy from Michigan State University. Her research of the past 2 decades has focused on equity and social justice in science education. Working within the intersection of formal/informal education, Calabrese Barton studies the design of teaching-learning environments and experiences that promote expansive learning outcomes, such as critical agency, identity work, and social transformation (as grounded within expanding disciplinary expertise). She also engages in participatory methodologies for embracing authentic research + practice work that attends to practitioner, youth and community members' voices, and critically engages the goals of equity and justice. Calabrese Barton is a Fellow of the American Education Research Association, and a WT Grant Distinguished Fellow. She recently was awarded the 2018 American Education Research Association Award for Exemplary Contributions to Practice-Engaged Research.

Edna Tan is associate professor of science education at the University of North Carolina at Greensboro. She has a PhD in science education from Teachers College, Columbia University. She takes a critical, sociocultural ethnographic approach in her work with youth and science teachers, both in the classroom, informal science programs, and across these spaces. Her work focuses on how youth from underrepresented backgrounds can be empowered to use science as a tool to address systemic injustice and to work with their teachers in creating transformative spaces for meaningful science engagement.

Note: The research in this book is supported in part by the National Science Foundation under Grant No. DRL-1421116. Any opinions, findings, and conclusions or recommendations expressed in this material are our own and do not necessarily reflect the views of the National Science Foundation.

The research in this book is also a reflection of the researchers, community partners, and youth who have collaborated together in these making spaces. We have learned so much from you and with you. A special thank you to Carmen Turner, Myunghwan Shin, Christina Restrepo Nazar, Day Greenberg, Sarah Keenan-Lechal, and ReAnna Roby in Michigan and Faith Brown-Freeman, Aerin Benavides, Lee Staton, and Grace Thompson in North Carolina.